THE STRATEGY
OF KNOWLEDGE

THE STRATEGY OF KNOWLEDGE

Warfare Strategies for Apostolic Leaders

LAURA HENRY HARRIS

XULON PRESS

Xulon Press
2301 Lucien Way #415
Maitland, FL 32751
407.339.4217
www.xulonpress.com

Unless otherwise indicated, Scripture quotations taken from the New King James Version (NKJV). Copyright © 1982 by Thomas Nelson, Inc. Used by permission. All rights reserved.

Printed in the United States of America.

ISBN: 9781545611623

Table of Contents

Dedication

In many ways this book has brought me full circle to the place where I began writing books years ago. The first book that I wrote, *True Wisdom Comes From God*, was never published. I had a nearly-complete manuscript before my mother passed away in 2003, but the book was never concluded. Knowing that she did not have long to live, my mother asked a dear friend to be a voice of encouragement to me to finish the book. In the process of finishing this book, *The Strategy of Knowledge,* I realized that the quest for knowledge, wisdom, and understanding was forming in my mind years ago when I wrote the first book. I realized as I read afresh the manuscript of the original work that my prayers for wisdom and knowledge have not significantly changed since that time.

I usually do not dedicate my writings to other people, wanting instead to give full glory to the Lord. In this case, however, I would like to honor my beloved parents, Dr. Charles and Laura Josephine "Jo" Henry, who were people full of sound wisdom and knowledge and who instilled a love of learning and discovery in me. I also want to honor Mrs. Dora Stone, a dear friend and spiritual mentor to me as a baby Christian. Mrs. Dora calls me a few times every year to ask if I have finished the first book. She knows that I have written other books, but her crucial assignment from my mother was to be a voice of encouragement to finish the original book that I began before my mother passed away. This book is a culmination, as much as anything can be culminated in the kingdom of God, of the original work. *The Strategy of Knowledge* has moved beyond the place of my original understanding, while also borrowing the themes that moved my heart back then. My desire throughout the lengthy span of that quest has been to seek the knowledge and wisdom of God to have a greater understanding of the things of his kingdom.

Section One

The Strategy of Knowledge

Call to Me, and I will answer you,
and show you great and mighty things,
which you do not know.

Jeremiah 33:3, NIV

Introduction

Years ago when I was reading in the book of Jeremiah, a verse jumped off the page to me. It was the first time that the Lord had given me the understanding that a particular verse had personal meaning for me. I read, "Call to Me, and I will answer you, and show you great and unsearchable things, which you do not know" (Jer. 33:3, NIV). I knew that I had stumbled upon a treasure that would be a life verse. I began to pray and claim the promise of Jeremiah 33:3 and sought to learn the hidden things of God. As the Lord began to teach me about knowledge, I began to have a greater understanding of the hidden strategies and discoveries of God that are looking for people to find them. I even wrote my first book, yet unpublished, about the wisdom of God.

The wisdom and knowledge of God are there for the taking and understanding. Well perhaps not completely, for the Lord is the one who reveals the hidden treasures that people do not yet know. However, he seeks people to seek him to be the receptacles of the treasures of wisdom and knowledge that have been hidden from the beginning of time. The Lord is no respecter of persons, and he will honor those who call to him with a pure heart and pure motives. He will show them unsearchable things, meaning he will reveal hidden matters which would not be found without the revelation of God. Here is a kernel of truth: The voice of the Lord is speaking, but most people are not hearing. Hear his words and know his voice. Believers should seek to know him as he knows us.

Knowledge: Currency of the Kingdom

The knowledge of the kingdom of God is not readily understood. People must learn about knowledge and how to seek it. There will always be those who will distort knowledge for the evil purposes of the enemy, but the Lord will use knowledge for his kingdom. Knowledge will increase survival chances as time goes on.

Because we live in the natural world, sometimes we look for monetary currency to live and survive. The currency of the kingdom of God is not money; kingdom currency is knowledge of the Lord! The book of Psalms says, "Teach me good judgment and knowledge, For I believe Your commandments. ...*The law of Your mouth is better to me than thousands of coins of gold and silver*" (Ps. 119:66,72). This is a huge breakthrough in understanding; let that soak in. Currency is exchange for exchange. The more we know of the Lord, the more that we will be able to exchange the situations of the world into the kingdom best. There is no need of money per se in the kingdom of God. There is no use for it. The Scriptures talk about the pavement being streets of gold in the heavenly realm. The things that are held in highest esteem on earth, such as gold, jewels, and pearls, are put under feet or are used for common building materials in God's realm. What use is there for money in the kingdom realm? Money is a function of living in the natural world; it is worthless in the kingdom of God. However, humanity does need it, even if for a season of time, until we are fully in the kingdom realm.

What is really valuable is knowledge of the Lord and understanding the opposite value of God's kingdom. In Luke 21, the widow gave two mites into the treasury of the temple. She put in more than all the others who gave more by worldly standards. She was operating on the currency of the heavenly realm - knowledge of honoring the Lord with all she had to offer.

> And He looked up and saw the rich putting their gifts into the treasury, and He saw also a certain poor widow putting in two mites. So He said, "Truly I say to you that *this poor widow has put in more than all*; for all these out of their abundance have

put in offerings for God, but she out of her poverty put in all the livelihood that she had." (Luke 21:1-4)

In other words, she put in all she had because she had a heart to put herself last and offer all she had to the Lord, not because of the great monetary value of her gift. The currency of her gift was knowledge and understanding of the Lord. The others were using currency standards of the world. In giving all she had, she put in the currency of the kingdom of heaven. If she had been in the world system, she would have kept her meager two mites to eat on, and then her worldly resources would have been gone. She declared her understanding of the Lord by dropping all she had into the bucket. We can suppose that he rewarded her with a kingdom reward. What the Lord is offering to believers and to the world is more precious than rubies or gold or silver or pearls. Knowledge of the Lord cannot be valued or measured in terms of the understanding of the world: "Therefore I love Your commandments more than gold, yes, than fine gold!" (Ps. 119:127).

Characteristics of Knowledge

Kingdom knowledge will be critical in the days ahead. Knowledge is the Lord's key to walking in the kingdom of God and overcoming the enemy. Knowledge is understanding God. It comes from the intimacy of relationship. There are some key characteristics of knowledge that will be addressed:

Knowledge is Fleeting

Knowledge may be seen as a momentary or passing opportunity. It may be attainable for those who seek it, but it will pass away for those who do not. It is present but unseen and unnoticed by those who do not know of its beauty and benefit. Knowledge will change the world, and in fact, it has already changed the world. The world will change more as more knowledge is revealed. There is some knowledge that is available now, but if not gained or understood, it may be lost. If it is not harvested in its season, it may be gone. Some knowledge has been lost by some only to be found by others.

There have been several times when the Lord has spoken something to me in a dream. One night I woke up with a very vivid memory. In a dream, I was on the front row of the studio audience at the Sid Roth show, "Its Supernatural." Before the taping started, Jesus, who was clothed in a white garment with a blue sash, walked in front of the audience to come straight to me. He leaned his head down to rest almost on my shoulder. He spoke something into my ear. It was a powerful message. It was a very important word that I knew was vitally important for me and many others to know. The next thing I knew was that I was sitting in the guest chair of the Sid Roth sound stage. Mr. Roth leaned in, as if hanging on my every word, and said, "What did he tell you?" I instantly woke up.

I thought about writing down the words of Jesus immediately in the middle of the night. However, in a semi-dazed state, I decided to write those precious words the next morning. That was a huge mistake! In the morning I remembered the dream, but I had no idea what Jesus had said to me because I could not remember. The knowledge was fleeting and I failed to grab hold of it when the opportunity presented itself. That was a few years ago. Since that time, I have often regretted the bad decision not to grab the knowledge when it was there ready to be taken.

The book of Luke recounts the story of Jesus weeping over Jerusalem: "Now as He drew near, He saw the city and wept over it, saying, '*If you had known*, even you, especially *in this your day*, the things that make for your peace! *But now they are hidden from your eyes*'" (Luke 19:41). The residents of Jerusalem had an opportunity to know, but when they failed to recognize the revelations of God, those things were then hidden from them. The knowledge was fleeting: When they did not recognize it, it was lost to them forever.

Knowledge is Revelatory

The Lord reveals himself in knowledge to people who are seekers. Seekers find the Lord and seekers know him. Non-seekers do not. Kingdom secrets from the foundation of the world are revealed to the seekers. The book of Matthew says, "All these things Jesus spoke to the multitude in parables; and without a parable He did not speak to them, that it might be fulfilled which was spoken by the prophet, saying: 'I will open my mouth in parables; I will utter things kept secret from the foundation of the world'" (Matt. 13:34-35). Furthermore, humanity can only know what God reveals about himself. History shows that God reveals himself to his special chosen ones, like Moses and Paul, and to others who are not so noteworthy. The revelations were great, but they were costly to the people who received them.

Knowledge is Exponential

The more a person knows the more a person can receive to know. To whom much is given, more will be given. The Lord will add to those who have already received, to give them more. Jesus said so in the book of Matthew:

> He answered and said to them, "*Because it has been given to you to know the mysteries of the kingdom of heaven*, but to them it has not been given. *For whoever has, to him more will be given, and he will have abundance*; but whoever does not have, even what he has will be taken away from him. (Matt. 13:11-12)

These verses are talking about knowledge of the kingdom of God! This is not talking about worldly gain or wealth or anything fleeting in the world system. Jesus spoke in riddles, or parables, so that those whose hearts were not pure would not see and understand the kingdom of God.

Knowledge is Quantitative

Global knowledge is added to daily. We have seen that throughout history. Each generation stands on the platform of the knowledge of those who have gone before. The book of Deuteronomy says, "The secret things belong to the Lord our God, but those things which are revealed belong to us and to our children forever, that we may do all the words of this law" (Deut. 29:29). It is also quantitative for individuals in their own understanding. The more one knows, the more he or she is able to comprehend.

Knowledge is Expansive and Infinite

Most people do not realize that knowledge is infinite. The Lord is forever increasing. To say otherwise would be to say that God is finite. No matter how vast God is, if there was an end to his presence and reign, then he would be finite. Therefore, as God is forever increasing, so too is the knowledge of him also forever increasing. Isaiah 9:7 says, "*Of the increase of His government and peace There will be no end*, Upon the throne of David and over His kingdom, to order it and establish it with judgment and justice from that time forward, even forever. The zeal of the Lord of hosts will perform this." Believers can never catch up to the speed of the growth of the expanse of God and his King's dominion, but we can know more than we know now on an exponential basis.

This book is divided into two parts. The first part of the book, *The Strategy of Knowledge*, is a study of the knowledge of God and his hidden blessings of knowledge that are available to believers who seek him. The second part, *Principles of War*, is about the warfare strategies that will help the body of Christ be more efficient in using the knowledge that we have to fight the enemy in an effective way. In many ways it may seem as if these topics are unrelated, but in actuality they are connected at the core of understanding God's kingdom and the warfare that will take place on earth to the end of days that will usher in God's kingdom. We cannot effectively battle the kingdom of darkness without the knowledge of God and without actual warfare strategies that will give us some tools for using that knowledge more effectively.

This book, *The Strategy of Knowledge*, is a companion book to the last book that I wrote entitled *Leader!* Both books are designed to guide apostolic leaders into greater understanding of the call to bring the Church into order so that we may strategically battle and fight the enemy unto victory.

Chapter 1

Understanding Knowledge

Some people say, "I am a person of one book," meaning that they will only read the Bible. That is fine, but that limited thinking severely diminishes the wealth of knowledge that those believers who have gone before have gained over the centuries. If each generation started from a point devoid of all known knowledge and gained only what they could gain from the Word, it could be that the generations would end basically at the same point of knowledge and understanding without advancing in discernment and revelation beyond the previous generations.

The truth is that each generation stands on the shoulders of the generations who have gone before. The ceiling of the immediate past generation is the floor of the current generation! Where the previous generation left off is where the next generation may begin its quest for knowledge and understanding. Known knowledge is beneficial knowledge. What is revealed to one generation is for the benefit of all future generations. The book of Deuteronomy says, "The secret things belong to the Lord our God, *but those things which are revealed belong to us and to our children forever*, that we may do all the words of this law" (Deut. 29:29). There is an ongoing cumulative effect of knowledge gained by those who have gone before. By way of example, consider how the apostles of the New Testament relied on the revelation of the prophets of the Old Testament.

Once a thing is known, it is likely to be known forever. However, there is no guarantee that *once-known* means *always-known*. Think of all the ancient things that puzzle modern day scientist or students of history as they try to figure out how certain things were done or made in antiquity. For example, Roman concrete has had durability that has left scientist baffled for centuries. There have been many studies to know what materials they used to make the concrete that was so durable and strong. In fact, what was developed 1,500 years ago is stronger than what is in use now. This is just one example of technology or formulas that have been lost over time.[1] It is important to guard the knowledge that we have been given.

All knowledge belongs to the Lord: "For the Lord is the God of knowledge" (1 Sam. 2:3). It is his to give. The book of Daniel says, "He reveals deep and secret things; He knows what is in the darkness, And light dwells with Him" (Dan. 2:22). The book of Romans says, "Oh, the depth of the riches both of the wisdom and knowledge of God! *How unsearchable are His judgments and His ways past finding out!*" (Rom. 11:33). The Lord gives knowledge to whom he pleases and to those who please him. According to Scripture, he loves when people seek him and want to know more about him and his hidden secrets. He gives his secrets to the righteous ones according to Scripture: "For the perverse person is an abomination to the LORD, but His secret counsel is with the upright" (Prov. 3:32).

The Lord can hide a matter or he can reveal a matter, which is clearly illustrated in Luke 24. There were two disciples on the road to Emmaus. At first their eyes were intentionally restrained by the Lord so that they did not know Jesus. The book of Luke says, "So it was, while they conversed and reasoned, that Jesus Himself drew near and went with them. *But their eyes were restrained, so that they did not know Him*" (Luke 24:15-16). Later however as they implored Jesus to stay with them to dine and fellowship, they knew him. Jesus opened their understanding: "Now it came to pass, as He sat at the table with them, that He took bread, blessed and broke it, and gave it to them. *Then their eyes were opened and*

---

[1] https://www.theguardian.com/science/2017/jul/04/why-roman-concrete-still-stands-strong-while-modern-version-decays Accessed July 6, 2017.

they knew Him; and He vanished from their sight" (Luke 24:30-31). Even later still, he met with the disciples in a closed room. He gave them divine revelation of Scriptures as he talked with them: "*He opened their understanding, that they might comprehend the Scriptures*" (Luke 24:45).

Hidden knowledge is not the same thing as secret knowledge by secret societies, which is evil. People who want to guard knowledge to be given only to a select few are not working in God's purposes. The Word of God says that there is nothing hidden that will not be revealed in its time (Mark 4:22). Hidden knowledge is talking about things that have been hidden by God but are released by God when it suits his purposes. People make themselves available to receive his knowledge. Seek more. It is good and it pleases God.

In fact, the early use of the word *knowledge* was as a verb meaning "to acknowledge or to recognize." Knowledge of God is to acknowledge God. Only later was the word *knowledge* used as a noun, meaning to have learning or gain understanding. As we acknowledge and recognize the Lord, knowledge and wisdom are sure to come.

The book of Jeremiah says, "Call to me and I will answer you and tell you great and unsearchable things you do not know" (Jer. 33:3, NIV). The relevance and magnitude of the implications of this verse are being made known. God answers to reveal deep and hidden things when people call to him. The ways of God are not revealed unless God reveals them. They are unsearchable without God moving to release revelation to people. Jeremiah 33:3

The Lord God hides things in his Word so that his people, at least the ones who are diligent, can find them: "It is the glory of God to conceal a matter, but the glory of kings is to search out a matter" (Prov. 25:2).

expanded through the lens of the original Hebrew language could be read this way: "Call (accost, hound, pester, pursue) to Me, and I will answer (pay attention or heed) you, and show (manifest or expose) you great (large and older) and mighty (isolated, hidden, unsearchable) things, which you do not know (ascertain by seeing, to know intimately)." Hounding and pestering the Lord is a sure way to *acknowledge and recognize* him, as stated above.

It is a worthy calling to want to know the hidden things of God. It appears that the Lord responds when people care enough about him and who he is to search out the secrets of his Word. The Lord God hides things in his Word so that his people, at least the ones who are diligent, can find them: "It is the glory of God to conceal a matter, but the glory of kings is to search out a matter" (Prov. 25:2). People do not usually rise to the level of being effective (glory filled) kings without having some wherewithal to be diligent and energetic. Indeed, we have the promise that all secrets will be revealed in due time. The book of Luke says, "For nothing is secret that will not be revealed, nor anything hidden that will not be known and come to light" (Luke 8:17). The Apostle Paul prayed in Ephesians 1, "Therefore I also, after I heard of your faith in the Lord Jesus and your love for all the saints, do not cease to give thanks for you, making mention of you in my prayers: that the God of our Lord Jesus Christ, the Father of glory, *may give to you the spirit of wisdom and revelation in the knowledge of Him, the eyes of your understanding being enlightened*" (Eph. 1:15-18). The wisdom, revelation, knowledge, and enlightenment referred to in Ephesians are grace gifts of God. He gives it. It is not received any other way.

For Christians in relationship with God, knowledge implies a relationship. For example, the Bible says that "Now Adam *knew* Eve his wife, and she conceived and bore Cain" (Gen. 4:1). The biblical euphemism *to know* means Adam had an intimate sexual union with his wife. Often in Scripture, *knowing* another meant intimacy in sexual union, which is the most intimate knowledge that people can have with one another.

The metaphor of knowing is used to describe the relationship of a believer with Jesus. Jesus used the Greek word *ginōskō*, which means "to know, to be aware of, have knowledge of, perceive, and understand." It may also refer to his saving relationship with those who follow Him: "I am the good shepherd; I *know* my sheep and my sheep *know* me" (John 10:14). He also told His disciples, "You will *know* the truth, and the truth will set you free" (John

8:32). The truth alone will not set anyone free; it is only the truth that a person *knows* that bring freedom. By contrast, Jesus said to the unbelieving Jews, "Yet you have not *known* (the Father), but I know Him" (John 8:55). Of course this is referring to intimacy, not of a sexual nature which is experienced in the flesh, but intimacy of an even greater potential. The deep intimacy of a person with the Holy Trinity. Unity with the Father, Jesus Christ, and the Holy Spirit is experienced in the spirit: The Holy Spirit of God and the spirit of humans.

Therefore, to *know* Jesus Christ is to experience him in a greater relationship than can be described in the human and limited understanding of sexual union. The Father gave marriage so that believers could have some point of reference of the love between him and his people. Holy and wholesome God-ordained marriage between a man and a woman, as intended by the Word of God, is the closest thing that is visible on earth to illustrate the relationship that the Lord is seeking with his people. Increasing in the knowledge of God is part of Christian growth and maturity. Christians are called to "*grow in the grace and knowledge* of our Lord and Savior Jesus Christ" (2 Pet. 3:18).

Knowledge is really about finding God and knowing his natures and attributes. It is about the revelation of his character. As a person begins to know him and is known by him, the relationship will grow. Knowledge is not about a body of learning or exchange of impartation of mere information. It may seem simplistic, but knowledge is about knowing God intimately. When there is knowing, there is an increase in the relationship. When there is a deepening of the relationship, knowledge increases.

Other Scriptures illustrate that knowledge of God is the basis of a relationship with him: "If you had known Me, you would have known My Father also; and from now on you know Him and have seen Him" (John 14:7); "But if anyone loves God, this one is known by Him" (1 Cor. 8:3), and also this verse, "Nevertheless the solid foundation of God stands, having this seal: 'The Lord knows those who are His'" (2 Tim. 2:19a). However, having knowledge of the Lord is not an absolute guarantee that the relationship with the Lord will continue if it is not nurtured: "But now after you have known God, or rather are known by God, how is it that you turn again to the weak and beggarly elements, to which you desire again to be in bondage?" (Gal. 4:9).

Once while I was on this quest of greater understanding, the Lord showed me the library of Heaven in a vision. He showed me in terms that I could understand. I was allowed to peer into the library and saw bookshelves with volumes of colored books. I could not see the end of the expanse of the volumes. The shelves went higher and wider than my eyes could see. The Lord said, "Laura, the hidden things, in fact the things in the library that you seek entry to, are found in the Word." The hidden things will only be revealed by the Father's direction, but he loves those who love his Word. Be a student of the Word. Psalm 119:105 says, "Your Word is a lamp to my feet and a light to my path." The Word illuminates the path, but the Word is not the path. In other words, the knowledge of God is too vast to be contained in the written Word of God, but we will not find the way to the vastness of God's potential for revelation and discernment without the guiding lamp of the Word of God to show the way to both our feet and his path. It is a three-part equation to find the way to revelation knowledge: His Word, our feet, and his path. The Word points in the right direction; his path and our steps have to be illuminated by the Word. We will find the way when the Word leads.

The Lord is the giver of knowledge, and he gives and he takes away. He is the source of the information. Knowledge will not begin or end with any person, but it is only a loan from the Lord for the advancement of the kingdom of God. The Lord further shared that he is in search of people to be receptacles of knowledge. The knowledge will be too vast for any one person. The Lord also told me, "When you felt dumb as a child or like you could not measure up, it was the enemy trying to get you to believe that you could not study and learn to show yourself approved." My confidence was very low as a child. I came in the shadow of brilliant people and I believed that my capacity to know and learn was sub-standard. Looking back, I often self-defeated just to get the agony of defeat out of the way. The end result is this: The Lord is the giver of knowledge and he will say who is blessed with understanding, but he is seeking those who are seeking him!

Vastness of Knowledge

The knowledge of God cannot be known by humanity on this side of heaven: "For now we see in a mirror, dimly, but then face to face. Now I know in part, but then I shall know just as I also am known" (1 Cor. 13:12). It appears that human beings have insufficient capacity to experience the kingdom of God, but even so humanity has much more mental capacity than has been utilized. The kingdom of God is forever expanding. So what is available today for knowledge will be surpassed by new revelation tomorrow. In other words, God is expanding all of the time, so the new things to be known about God tomorrow are greater than the things that can be known about him today. Isaiah 9:7 says, "*Of the increase* of his government and peace *there will be no end.*" The perpetual expansion of his government is the never-ending increase of his kingdom and dominion. Isaiah talks of a day when the Messiah will reign and the result will be that, "the earth shall be full of the knowledge of the Lord as the waters cover the sea" (Isa. 11:9).

The Lord said, "Worship me. Learn more about me. Focus your focus." This gives understanding that to grow more, we focus on him and delight in him. As the children of God begin to study the vastness of his knowledge, it soon becomes apparent that it is indeed beyond comprehension and it is truly unsearchable. It seems apparent that the Lord wants to give his children more, but people must want it enough to seek it. The book of John supports the notion that the knowledge of the acts of God is beyond our most expansive imaginations. It says, "And there are also many other things that Jesus did, which if they were written one by one, I suppose that even the world itself could not contain the books that would be written. Amen" (John 21:25). This is biblical support that the knowledge that is available cannot be contained. This is not merely talking about the acts of Jesus while he was on the earth for a few years. I understand this to mean the acts of an eternal and ever expanding God!

The revelation of knowledge is based on the genuineness of a person's heart for the Lord. Solomon said in Ecclesiastes: "For God gives wisdom and knowledge and joy to a man who is good in His sight" (Eccles. 2:26). True knowledge comes from the Word of God and the internal revelation of God in a person's heart. Knowledge comes from having the Father reveal to the person things that have been hidden since the foundation of the world. Even now, there is more that is still hidden than has been revealed to this point in history.

In the end, when people are with the Lord in heaven, the need for knowledge will pass away. All knowledge will then be known. All will be fully known then, just as we are fully known (1 Cor. 13:12). Each person will be known fully. The Lord knows everything already. There is nothing that is news to the Lord. Each one will be fully known as we are known and each will know fully. That means that no knowledge will be withheld then as it is now. The human capacity to know now is severely limited, but the full capacity of the human mind has not been revealed even now. There is so much more that each person could receive if the mind was properly opened to the Lord and his will.

As time goes on, knowledge will increase. The Word says so in Daniel 12:4: "But you, Daniel, shut up the words, and seal the book until the time of the end; *many shall run to and fro, and knowledge shall increase*." Many people have thought that meant an explosion of information. In fact, there has been an explosion of information. Even thinking back to the time of the beginning of the twentieth century, consider all the things that were not yet discovered or invented. The expansion of knowledge in the last 150 years has been incredible. It seems that the more that is known, the more it opens the possibility of the expansion of even more knowledge. But also consider that the explosion of information is a natural phenomenon that is indicative of what is happening in the spiritual world. Knowledge of both good and evil has increased. The explosion of inventions and understanding on the earth illustrates what is happening in the heavenly realms.

The tree of the knowledge of good and evil was tapped into in Eden. It was not a tree of good and evil; it was a tree of knowledge.

The fruit of that tree has been growing on the earth since that time. What are some good things of knowledge? Think of penicillin, for example. It is a substance that cures the body from infections, but it is born out of mold. Mold is evidence of uncleanness in Leviticus: "If the mold has spread in the fabric, the woven or knitted material, or the leather, whatever its use, *it is a persistent defiling mold; the article is unclean*" (Lev. 13:51). The substance that is unclean is used for good to cure many people of infections that could kill. That is one example of something that is bad that is used for a greater good; it is good and bad mixed together. What Satan intended for harm, mold and a curse, was apprehended for good.

Knowledge is a kernel of truth that will grow into a massive tree. The level of knowledge has been just barely tapped. There is a mud puddle that appears by our creek after a heavy rain. The Lord spoke to me one day and used that puddle as an example. He said that the puddle of about ten feet in diameter represented all of the known knowledge. The other hidden and unknown knowledge is represented by all of the waters of the world. (And actually even more than that because knowledge is always increasing because God is always increasing.) God is not finite. The waters of the world are finite. It would be a difficult task, but all the waters could be measured. Humanity cannot even begin to understand the vastness of the wealth of knowledge that is available. Solomon aptly described the quest for knowledge when he wrote: "And I set my heart to seek and search out by wisdom concerning all that is done under heaven; this burdensome task God has given to the sons of man, by which they may be exercised.... And I set my heart to know wisdom and to know madness and folly. I perceived that this also is grasping for the wind" (Eccles. 1:13,17).

Chapter 2

Wisdom from the Holy Spirit

The Lord gives people knowledge by the power of the Holy Spirit. The Spirit of God carries all knowledge. Paul taught the Corinthians about the wisdom that comes from God in 1 Corinthians. Paul shared about wisdom that was not of the world. He said, "But we speak the wisdom of God in a mystery, *the hidden wisdom which God ordained before the ages for our glory*, which none of the rulers of this age knew; for had they known, they would not have crucified the Lord of glory" (1 Cor. 2:7-8). God has mysteries to be revealed that were known before the ages began, but which are only revealed by the direction of God. Paul further quoted Isaiah 64:4 when he said, "Eye has not seen, nor ear heard, nor have entered into the heart of man the things *which God has prepared for those who love him*" (1 Cor. 2:9). The blessing of that statement is that the mysteries of God are for those who love the Lord. Those people who are in an intimate relationship with the Lord will receive knowledge by the power of the Holy Spirit.

This means that there are things that devoted, faithful people will receive by revelation that others will not. Those mysteries are only discerned by a relationship with the Spirit of God and come by the Holy Spirit into the hearts of humanity. Paul said, "But God has revealed them to us through His Spirit. For the Spirit searches all things, *yes, the deep things of God*. For what man knows the things of a man except the spirit of the man which is in him? *Even so no one knows the things of God except the Spirit of God"* (1 Cor. 2:10-11). Because the Spirit of God is the only one who knows the deep and unsearchable mysteries of God, the Holy Spirit is the source of all revelation.

The very reason that we are given the blessing of the comforting, edifying, and counseling Holy Spirit is that we might know the things that God wants us to know. The Holy Spirit is the conduit of manifestation and revelation of God into the hearts and minds of people. The revelation is not just wisdom, but to reveal God himself to humanity to the extent that people can receive and process those revelations. Paul said, "Now we have received, not the spirit of the world, but the Spirit who is from God, *that we might know the things that have been freely given to us by God"* (1 Cor. 2:12). The wisdom of man will never be enough to receive the things of the Lord. The carnal man will never understand the things of the Spirit for they are spiritually discerned: "These things we also speak, not in words which man's wisdom teaches but which the Holy Spirit teaches, comparing spiritual things with spiritual. *But the natural man does not receive the things of the Spirit of God, for they are foolishness to him; nor can he know them, because they are spiritually discerned"* (1 Cor. 2:13-14).

Knowledge is the key because it has the potential to open doors and unlock information that holds all solutions to all problems. It is impossible for humanity to unlock mysteries without the guidance of the Holy Spirit. With the guidance of the Holy Spirit, the potential is there to open up new arenas and avenues of understanding. Knowledge comes with a call, and the infilling

Knowledge comes with a call, and the infilling of the Holy Spirit comes with a purpose for the kingdom of God. Knowledge given by God is for the benefit of the common good.

comes with a purpose for the kingdom of God. Knowledge given by God is for the benefit of the common good. What is received from the Lord must be shared for the overall good of the advancement of the kingdom of God on the earth!

Knowledge and Relationship

There are some who have a relationship with the Lord but do not have knowledge. Some people merely want to be close to the Lord, but do not know that the relationship opens doors that mere learning does not. There are people who merely want to be in the presence of the Lord but do not seek to know more. There are also those who have head "knowledge" but do not have a relationship with the Lord. Actually knowledge and relationship go together, but they are not the same things.

There are some biblical examples of the difference between knowledge and relationship: Peter had both relationship and knowledge in due time. Relationship without mature understanding did not yield as much for the kingdom as Peter did when he was mature in relationship and understanding. Knowledge and relationship operating together allowed boldness and strategy that he did not have when he had relationship with Jesus, albeit an immature relationship. The infilling of the Holy Spirit allowed him to speak with unction that caused over 3000 people to come to the Lord. The power and strategy came from the Holy Spirit. Before that time, Peter was in relationship, but there was no power.

Also, think of Paul and his presentation of the Gospel. Paul was often single-minded. He had a personality that caused him to push and be zealous for whatever team he was playing for at the time. Paul was a tremendous student of the Old Testament Scriptures. He was a star pupil, but he did not intimately know the subject matter of the prophecies that pointed to the Messiah. Paul had *book-learning* at first, also known as the wisdom of men, but he had no relationship. When Paul encountered the Risen Savior on the road to Damascus (Acts 9) and then went to Arabia for three years, the relationship with the Lord was formed (Gal. 1:17-18).

During that three-year absence, there was some question if Paul was in Arabia, or in the wilderness, or both. In the Septuagint, the Greek translation of the Old Testament the word used was *araba*, meaning "wilderness or sterile place." Either way, Paul was transformed by the time that he reemerged from his hiatus! He was a different person than he was when he left. He reemerged from blackout with a fully formed theology that could only be gained from the Holy Spirit. In fact, Paul said that what he knew was not taught by men. He said, "But I make known to you, brethren, that the gospel which was preached by me is not according to man. For I neither received it from man, nor was I taught it, *but it came through the revelation of Jesus Christ*" (Gal. 1:11-12).

At that point, it appeared that the learned knowledge of Paul was apprehended and used by the Holy Spirit. His formal education was used as a platform upon which to place the revelation knowledge of God. His human understanding of Old Testament Scriptures was used by the Holy Spirit to allow him to teach and bridge the gap from the Old Testament understanding to the Gospel message of Jesus as the Messiah. Because he had human knowledge and understanding, the Spirit could use that to open new revelation so that he could then teach the people about how the Old Testament Scriptures pointed to Jesus. A person who did not have the thorough knowledge of the Jewish laws and traditions could not have been used as effectively by the Holy Spirit. Paul was the perfect teacher for Jews, Gentiles, and kings (Acts 9:15). His relationship with Jesus and his knowledge of Israel's Scriptures, history, and traditions allowed him to be a strategic general in God's army. He was uniquely situated to use his learning to illustrate to all people the truth of the Lord Jesus as the long-awaited Messiah that the Jews had been seeking. He could also educate the Gentiles about the history of the Jews that pointed to Jesus as the Savior, not only of Israel but also of the nations.

Knowledge is the intimate understanding that unlocks the mysteries of the kingdom of God. Knowledge is power. Knowledge is easy to the one who perceives. When there is perception of who God is in intimacy, knowledge and wisdom come on its heels. By knowing the Lord intimately, revelations are given which include strategy and deeper understanding of the truth. A child may understand the truth, but a theologian may miss the mark. Knowledge of the truth is the thing that separates mere learning from the intimacy of revelation. Some know Scriptures but do not know the Savior. It is hard to imagine, but it is true. Knowledge is intimate learning and understanding. Revelation of the Lord comes from intimacy in

31

seeking to know him more and being a willing vessel. True knowledge of God comes from relationship.

The Lord said to me, "You have loved intimacy for a long time and some knowledge has been born out of that, but this is the time that you are very hungry to know more - not for your own good, but for my kingdom." Some can have intimacy without knowledge, but no one can have the deep and revealed knowledge of God without intimacy. *To know* means intimacy in the marital sense, which is a deep, private knowing that occurs between two lovers that only they know and experience together. The understanding of the word *intimate* includes themes like guarded, innermost, secret, confidential, profound, deep, close, comfortable, cherished, or near. May we pray this prayer with conviction:

Dear Lord,

These descriptive words are what I want in a relationship with you. I know in my heart that the level of relationship with you is up to me. You are waiting for intimacy with those who will seek it. God, I am seeking a deeper and more intimate walk with you. I know that it will be a process, but Lord I am praying to be in it for the long haul. Lord, I want to know you in a way that few do. I am hungry for a love relationship that many will not find because they do not know to seek it.

I am praying that I can teach many to seek that kind of relationship with you. Dear Lord, I love you, and I want to love you more. I am seeking a deeper and more abiding love. Lord, help me to seek you with truth in my heart.

Please help me to love you more than I love my sins. Help me to prune the dead wood, so that I can get close to you. I know that in my sins I can only get to a certain level with you. I am praying that I

can be more Christlike in my ways and thoughts.
The more I become like you, the more I know you
intimately! Lord, help me. Amen.

In other words, the more the Lord is allowed to reign in a
person, the more revelation that person will have in intimacy. The
more he is Lord of a person's life, the more that person will know
the Lord because of personal experience. As a person yields his or
her will, the knowledge will come from within by the revelation
of the Holy Spirit. Knowledge is actually experiencing God from
within. Breakthrough comes because people want to know the Lord
more. The hunger is strong enough to cause them to put aside those
things that hinder a deeper relationship with him. Knowledge is
revelation of God, but it comes because people are seeking to be
made perfect in love and be more like him. Philippians 1:9 illustrates that revelation is born out of love and the primary mode
of operation is in the abounding of love: "And this I pray: that
your love may abound yet more and more and extend to its fullest
development in knowledge and all keen insight (that your love may
display itself in greater depth of acquaintance and *more compre-
hensive discernment*)" (Phil. 1:9, AMP).

God does not limit himself in the lives of people; people limit
God. He is not one way to some people and one way to others. God
is God and the level of what a person knows and understands of
him and his ways is directly dependent on what each person seeks
to know about him. Knowledge of God is directly dependent on
what a person wants to know. Love and intimacy invite him. God
is everywhere. Either a person believes that he is everywhere or he
is not. He is! If God is everywhere, he already knows every sinner
intimately. However, God is not revealed until a person opens the
door and accepts the Lord, who will then reveal his presence in that
person's life. God may pursue a person, but deep and true knowledge of God comes in the formation of the relationship between
that person and the Lord.

The question is this: Do we want to crush the flesh so that we
can know the Lord more? Are we willing to overcome distractions
and circumstances to be devoted to him? Can we love the Lord and

be intimate with him in any situation? We must cultivate that and pray to cultivate it more. The more carnal, flesh junk that a person has hidden deep inside, the less that person can know of the hidden things of God. Understanding yielded submission actually unlocks a huge part of the mystery of knowledge. Knowledge is actually a function of yielded submission. The more a person yields to the Lord, the more the Lord will be on the throne of his or her life and the more that person will know the Lord.

It is like drilling an oil well: Until a person yields to the process of drilling, fracking, and pumping, and until the oil is actually visible, the grade, color, or pungent nature of the oil is not known. The oil was there all along, but it cannot be experienced until a person takes the necessary steps to acquire it. Oil is hidden until someone seeks to find and reveal it. Its qualities are not known until it is actually found. If a person does not seek it, it will not be found. A person does not stumble on oil; it is pursued. Discovery of oil does not happen by happenstance; it is found only by great effort. The same is mostly true of the Lord and a relationship with him. Intimacy pulls back the veil to knowledge. The veil, once removed, reveals the hidden natures of God.

The book of Hosea says, "My people are destroyed for lack of knowledge. *Because you have rejected knowledge, I also will reject you* from being priest for Me; Because you have forgotten the law of your God, I also will forget your children" (Hosea 4:6). Rejection of knowledge is a serious thing to the Lord. It pleases God when we pursue him by pursuing the knowledge of him: "Let us know, *let us pursue the knowledge of the Lord.* His going forth is established as the morning; He will come to us like the rain, Like the latter and former rain to the earth" (Hosea 6:3). Hosea also illustrates that God desires that his people seek knowledge of him: "For I desire mercy and not sacrifice, And *the knowledge of God more than burnt offerings*" (Hosea 6:6). These verses seem to go along with the idea that knowledge is intimate understanding and relationship with the Lord. Indeed, people are destroyed for lack of knowing God. The pursuit of the knowledge of the Lord is strategic because it opens a person to receive the revelation of his thoughts and his strategies.

Chapter 3

Knowledge, Strategies, and Witty Inventions

I have a friend and colleague in my seminary studies who was an engineer before entering the ministry. He and a coworker had worked on a challenging engineering problem for months. No matter how hard they searched and thought about the matter, they could not find the solution to the problem. One day as he was shaving, he uttered a simple prayer about the matter. The Lord dropped the solution into his mind. With shaving cream on his face, he quickly jotted down the solution on a piece of paper. He took the paper to his partner, without telling him where he had received the answer. The coworker said that there was no way that the given solution would work. My friend asked him to give it a try anyway. The coworker came back and said, "There is no way that this should work, but it did." The Lord provided the solution and strategy that the men could not find with months of effort and searching on their own. The answer appeared to be unsearchable by their human efforts.

Most people do not know that there are secrets of God that are begging to be discovered and most do not seek the Lord in that way. Strategies of God, witty inventions, and discoveries are just revelations of what were there all along. All elements of matter are in existence in one form or another and have been since creation.

All elements needed to fabricate a vehicle were present during the Stone Age, but people did not have the revelation of how to formulate a vehicle at that time, or even know how to extract the fuel from the earth that would be necessary for its operation. There is really no such thing as an invention in terms of creation. There are only new discoveries of how to use the resources that God has put at the disposal of humanity. In other words, new things are not really created, they are only repurposed from old things. People cannot make something out of nothing. They take those things that God has given to humanity and formulate them to be something useful.

Proverbs says, "It is the glory of God to conceal a matter, but the glory of kings is to search out a matter" (Prov. 25:2). God wants to reveal, but most of the discoveries are not stumbled upon, but rather sought after. What that means is that most discoveries are pursued, not handed over on a silver platter. The *hint of a discovery* may be stumbled upon or given in a dream. The interest of a person may be piqued by some observation or revelation, but then the person must act on the information given by God. This is true of Sir Isaac Newton, who had the hint of a discovery in the moment that he saw an apple fall to the ground. If he had not pursued that line of thought, he would not have discovered the law of gravity. He did not create gravity; he merely had revelation of what was there all along. If a person does not pursue the conclusion of the idea, the idea will not come to a fruitful end.

Ecclesiastes 1:9 says, *"That which has been is what will be, that which is done is what will be done, and there is nothing new under the sun."* All the answers to all questions and problems are available for discovery. All solutions to all problems are already in existence. In the vastness of God's power and presence there are no insurmountable problems; for if there were, then God would not be all powerful. Therefore, it makes sense to read Ecclesiastes 1:9 to say, "That which has been (in heaven) is what will be (on earth), that which is done (in heaven) is what will be done (on earth)" (explanatory notes added). The Lord God has already formulated everything, and all uses of materials have been available from the beginning. There is indeed nothing new under the sun.

Each generation builds on the shoulders of the knowledge of the generations that have gone before. The strategies sought by the current generation for end time management are all there. The witty inventions are all there, begging for discovery. The knowledge of the Lord, which is the manifestation of the Lord, wants to be seen, known, and noticed. The Lord loves to reveal himself when the appointed time is right. Things of the Lord have not failed to be revealed because the Lord necessarily wants them to be hidden, but because the timing of God is not ripe, or people are not ready or willing to receive the discoveries. When people get prepared, open, and receptive, the Lord shows them what they can take and are ready to receive. He will show people what he wants them to know, but each one has to be ready. He could have shown a caveman a vision of an automobile, but his generation was not ready to act on the revelation. This makes me think of the visions of Ezekiel 1. Could it be that Ezekiel had a vision of some future flying aircraft that he had no paradigm to understand or explain? It is like showing a caveman a vision of a car and asking him to describe it to his caveman friends in caveman terms.

In the proper time, the Lord will show knowledge to those who seek to know the answers. The main objectives of this book are to reveal to people the possibility of receiving such knowledge and to stimulate enthusiasm in people to go after God for the revelation of his hidden treasures. Most will not care or will not seek. The Lord will give anyone this understanding of knowledge who dares to press in to know more. Human effort also plays a significant role. Mostly, it appears that people are gifted with revelation in areas they have studied, learned, and about which they have greater understanding. They give the Lord something to work with in giving them the revelations. However, it can also happen that revelations may be given to a person who has no basis for understanding. I have heard of a highly technical chemical formula being given by God to a person who is not a chemist. That is more challenging, not for God, but for humanity.

The answers are right in front of God's people. Sometimes the Lord gives strategy on the simple things that make life much easier. My husband is an attorney. A few times in his legal career, the Lord has prompted him to research an obscure legal theory, which led to discovery of information so that he could win a case or receive a larger settlement than he otherwise would have received. When he knew to look for something hidden or obscure by the grace of God, he did not create the answer; he merely found what was there all along. There is a godly solution for every situation under the sun. They are all there, and the Lord is saying by his Word, "LOOK FOR THEM!"

Solutions, Inventions, and Blueprints in the Word of God

The Lord has given knowledge, strategies, and witty inventions throughout biblical and human history. Even early in the book of Genesis, the Lord started giving divine revelation to lead and guide his people. The Lord is indeed the giver of solutions for problems that appear to be unsolvable. The solutions that appear on the pages of Scripture are incredible. Moving forward through history some of the inventions and discoveries that are most helpful for humanity were inspired by God.

In Genesis 6, the Lord gave Noah the exact specifications for the ark. Noah was righteous and he walked in divine grace. He was given a plan to save himself and his family, but he had to act on what the Lord told him or he would have perished along with the rest of humanity. This illustrates that the Lord will give plans and strategies for salvation to protect his people from harm for God's purposes. It also reveals that there is a human component to the implementation of divine strategies. If people know to look and seek, the Lord will make provision for them by giving ideas directly from his throne of grace. The Lord gave Noah knowledge of the future so he could be prepared for what was coming.

The Lord gave Joseph knowledge about the severe famine that would strike the world. Before that, however, the works of his hands prospered and there were collateral blessings for his masters. The Lord was with Joseph, and he was successful in all he did. As he was in the house of his master, Potiphar, the Bible says, "So it was, from the time that he had made him overseer of his house and all that he had, that *the Lord blessed the Egyptian's house for*

Joseph's sake; and the blessing of the Lord was on all that he had in the house and in the field" (Gen. 39:5). Later, in the prison, the Word also reveals, "The keeper of the prison did not look into anything that was under Joseph's authority, *because the Lord was with him; and whatever he did, the Lord made it prosper*" (Gen. 39:23). Joseph was blessed in his master's house, in the prison, and in the court of a king. Others were blessed by his favor from God, which were collateral blessings.

Solomon's wisdom exceeded any wisdom known before or after. First Kings 10:24 states "all the earth" sought the wisdom of Solomon. Solomon wrote in Proverbs 8:12 that it was "wisdom" (which God gave him in an unprecedented amount) which produces discoveries. It says, "I wisdom dwell with prudence, and *find out knowledge of witty inventions*" (Prov. 8:12). The Queen of Sheba came to test his wisdom, and it was beyond her greatest expectation. She must have been a student of wisdom and knowledge even to be interested in the level of Solomon's wisdom and knowledge. Second Chronicles 9:2 says, "So Solomon answered all her questions; there was nothing so difficult for Solomon that he could not explain it to her."

Solomon's quest for keen understanding was for the greater good of his people. He prayed to the Lord saying, "Now give me wisdom and knowledge, that I may go out and come in before this people; for who can judge this great people of Yours?" (2 Chron. 1:10). Solomon's request pleased the Lord:

> Because this was in your heart, and you have not asked riches or wealth or honor or the life of your enemies, nor have you asked long life—but have asked wisdom and knowledge for yourself, that you may judge My people over whom I have made you king—wisdom and knowledge are granted to you; and I will give you riches and wealth and honor, such as none of the kings have had who were before you, nor shall any after you have the like. (2 Chron. 1:11-12)

Daniel teaches that God is the revealer of mysteries. He sought the Lord for the revelation of the mysteries of the king's dream. Daniel was not defiled by his circumstances in the pagan Babylonian kingdom. He sought the Lord to gain understanding. He did not give up until the answer came. The book of Daniel says, "Then Daniel went to his house, ... *that they might seek mercies from the God of heaven concerning this secret, ... Then the secret was revealed to Daniel in a night vision. ...* He gives wisdom to the wise and knowledge to those who have understanding. *He reveals deep and secret things*" (Dan. 2:17-22, selections).

Cyrus, the king of the Persians, was called later to overthrow the Babylonian kingdom. His ultimate purpose of God was to free the Israelites who had been in captivity for seventy years in Babylon (Jer. 25:12). By the words of the prophet Isaiah, the Lord called Cyrus by name about 150 years before his reign. (Isa. 44:27-45:5). Historical accounts support the idea that Cyrus had divine revelation of how to enter the seemingly impregnable fortress of Babylon. His entry came at just the right time to fulfill the prophecies to allow captive Israel to return to Jerusalem at the end of the Babylonian captivity. Tradition is that he knew by revelation knowledge to divert the waters of the Euphrates River. The gates did not protect from what should have been an under-water entry. As the diverted waters receded from around the fortress, an opening to the city was exposed. His army then walked into the city on the dry river bed.

There were many more instances of divine revelation of strategy and knowledge on the pages of Scripture. Moses received the exact dimension and structure of the tabernacle, including all of the accouterments used for worship. The Lord gave Joshua, Gideon, David, and Jehoshaphat warfare strategies that would have been impossible in the natural realm. He gifted artisans of the tabernacle and temple to make the articles to his exact specifications. The king of Tyre sent Solomon, "a skillful man, endowed with understanding, ... skilled to work in gold and silver, bronze and iron, stone and wood, purple and blue, fine linen and crimson, and to make any engraving *and to accomplish any plan which may be given to him...*" (2 Chron. 13-14, selections). There were many other instances in the Word about people receiving revelations of knowledge and information that fit into God's plans and purposes.

Other Believers Who Understood Knowledge

Many of the world's greatest scientists, musicians, and inventors believed the Word of God and credited their incredible discoveries to the Lord. Part of what has moved the heart of God in revealing knowledge in the past has been the selfless nature of people who are looking to gain information for the greater good of God's kingdom or humanity. When God's people embrace the call to the common good more fully, it will aid in their pursuit of knowledge. They have been blessed to find out knowledge

Part of what has moved the heart of God in revealing knowledge in the past has been the selfless nature of people who are looking to gain information for the greater good of God's kingdom or humanity. When God's people embrace the call to the common good more fully, it will aid in their pursuit of knowledge.

of witty inventions as revealed in Proverbs 8:12.

Sir Isaac Newton discovered gravity and formulated laws of motion. His search to understand God's methods and order of the universe led to many of his discoveries. Newton said, "All variety of created objects which represent order and life in the universe could happen only by the willful reasoning of its original Creator, whom I call the 'Lord God.'"[2] Newton also said, "In the absence of any other proof, the thumb alone would convince me of God's existence."[3]

Scientist George Washington Carver was a student of the common peanut. He discovered over three hundred uses for it and its byproducts. Carver did not create anything; he merely discovered what was right before him, and everyone else for that matter. He was born a slave but found freedom at the end of the Civil War.

---

[2]   https://www.brainyquote.com/quotes/quotes/i/isaacnewto753049.html. Accessed May 4, 2017.

[3]   https://www.goodreads.com/quotes/search?utf8. Accessed May 4, 2017.

He prayed to the Lord and asked that he might know the secrets of the universe. The Lord responded to him and said, "Little man, you are too small to grasp the secrets of the universe. But I will show you the secret of the peanut."[4] He listened and he sought, and the Lord showed him secrets by divine revelation.

Carver was not special, other than he followed and pursued a desire to know what God knows. He was looking for solutions to help the people survive in the war-ravaged South after the Civil War. Carver said, "The secret of my success? It is simple. It is found in the Bible. I prayed that my life and work had helped in a small way to make the world peaceful and make Him happy." He was referred to as man's slave who became God's scientist.[5] Carver took no books into his laboratory, which he called "God's Little Workshop." If a person was seeking to learn a secret that had been previously hidden, it would not be written in a book anyway!

History is full of inventions that God downloaded to men and women through dreams, visions, and just plain wild ideas. For example, here are some things God downloaded in dreams alone: Mendeleyev created the periodic table; Frederick A. von Kekule solved the structural riddle of the benzene molecule (a closed carbon ring) from a dream in which he saw a snake seizing its own tail; Frederick Banting isolated insulin; Elias Howe finished his lock-stitch sewing machine; Einstein developed the theory of relativity; and Handel heard the last movement of the great masterpiece *Messiah*.[6] The conclusion of Handel's *Messiah* sounds like a choir of angels singing with heights and depths of vocal ranges that reach the outside levels of human capabilities. God spoke to Solomon in a dream for him to ask for anything he wanted when Solomon asked for wisdom and knowledge (1 Kings 3:5). Dreams have been critical for downloading information to people throughout Scripture.

---

[4] http://www1.cbn.com/ChurchWatch/archive/2010/05/17/the-legacy-of-george-washington-carver. Accessed April 11, 2017.

[5] http://righthandofgod.com/oneonone/pdf/Petition%20for%20Witty%20Inventions.pdf Accessed April 14, 2017.

[6] http://www.fromhispresence.com/radical-prayer-3-wild-ideas-witty-inventions Accessed April 14, 2017.

Other people who had tremendous world changing discoveries confessed a firm belief in God. Joseph Lister, who was the founder of antiseptic surgery said, "I am a believer in the fundamental doctrines of Christianity." Louis Pasture, who developed pasteurization and immunizations said, "The more I study nature, the more I stand amazed at the work of the Creator." Blaise Pascal, who worked in hydrodynamics and calculations, said, "How can anyone lose who chooses to be a Christian? If, when he dies, there turns out to be no God and his faith was in vain, he has lost nothing--in fact, has been happier in life than his non-believing friends. If, however, there is a God and a heaven and hell, then he has gained heaven and his skeptical friends will have lost everything in hell!" Wilbur and Orville Wright were great inventors and devout, Bible-believing Christians. They drew inspiration from creation and carefully studied the flight of birds and the Word of God in making some of their discoveries.[7]

Christopher Columbus felt that God wanted him to explore the world and find new lands and peoples so that Christ could be proclaimed. He was often ridiculed for his beliefs. Columbus wrote, "At this time I both read and studied all kinds of literature: cosmography, histories, chronicles, and philosophy and other arts, to which our Lord opened my mind unmistakably to the fact that it was possible to navigate from here to the Indies, and He evoked in me the will for the execution of it." In a letter to the monarchs of Spain dated July 7, 1503, Columbus records hearing a divine voice declaring, "Since thou wast born, ever has He [God] had thee in His watchful care," and also that when he had reached an age which pleased God he heard, "Of the barriers of the Ocean Sea, which were closed with such mighty chains, He gave thee the key."[8]

The final quote revealed that Columbus heard from God that the way had been barred before. Perhaps it was not the right time in God's plan. Columbus was given the divine revelation to make his epic journey to the New World. Also consider this: Columbus

---

[7]   http://righthandofgod.com/oneonone/pdf/Petition%20for%20Witty%20Inventions.pdf Accessed April 14, 2017.

[8]   https://www.goodreads.com/quotes/search/Christopher/Columbus Accessed May 4, 2017.

positioned himself to be available for the divine download from God by being a veteran and equipped sea captain. He had the skills which could be used by God for such a task.[9] He was in position for such a time as that time.

Sir James Simpson discovered the properties of chloroform for anesthesiology. He was inspired by Adam's deep sleep as a rib was removed from his side to form Eve. During an interview, he was asked, "'Sir, what do you consider your greatest discovery?' Sir James replied, 'My greatest discovery was when I discovered I was a sinner in the sight of God.' The newspaper man tried again: 'Thank you, Sir James. And now would you please tell me your second greatest discovery.' 'By all means,' replied that great Christian. 'My second greatest discovery was when I discovered that Jesus died for a sinner like me.'"[10]

The Source

The Lord is with his people as they pray and study the Word. The Word is the source of all knowledge that people are seeking from God. The Lord wants his people to know mysteries and the opening of the solutions are in the Word. The Word is the key to unlocking the mysteries of God. All revelation must line up with the Word of God. People must learn the potential of pursuit. This book is to teach people how to pursue knowledge about what

---

[9] The Lord will use whatever gifts and graces are made available to him when a person decides to live in yielded submission to him. I have always known that the skills that I used practicing law were preparation for what the Lord is allowing me to do now. The twenty years that I practiced law as an attorney were not wasted; they were merely groundwork for my later service to the Lord. This is also seen in Joseph's service to the Lord (Gen. 37-50). His preparation in slavery and in prison was hard, but there was no university for management in ancient Egypt. He learned skills in those hard settings that were useful to him when he walked fully into his call to save Israel from famine and destruction. Do not despise beginnings that do not appear to serve any kingdom function because the Lord can use all preparations for the greater good of his kingdom.

[10] http://christianevidences.org/scientific-evidence/anesthesiololgy/relevant-pioneer-quotes/ Accessed May 4, 2017.

interests them or about what God has put on their hearts. God has given each person gifts and graces that can be areas where revelation and knowledge are given.

Another example of knowledge that may be pursued is when a person has overcome an obstacle in his or her life. For example, a person who has been delivered of a burden, hindrance, bondage, such as depression or drug addiction, may have greater revelation of helping others overcome those matters than a person who has not experienced them. If a person who is actively struggling with depression or drug addiction, for example, would pursue those topics as an area of knowledge from the Lord, that person is more likely to overcome those hindrances in his or her life and help many others to overcome as well. It often comes down to using the knowledge for the greater good of God's kingdom on earth.

The Holy Spirit gift of knowledge is often misunderstood too. Many people think that a gift of knowledge is revelation of a condition for physical healing (1 Cor. 12:8). The gift of knowledge, like every spiritual gift, is revelation for the greater good: "But the manifestation of the Spirit is *given to each one for the profit of all*" (1 Cor. 12:7). The gift of knowledge can have the benefit of helping one person get delivered or healed, but it can also be for revelation of solutions to problems that benefit all people: "And though I have the gift of prophecy, *and understand all mysteries and all knowledge,* and though I have all faith, so that I could remove mountains, but have not love, I am nothing" (1 Cor. 13:2). This verse illustrates that knowledge pursued is unimportant except that it is grounded in love. The Lord is seeking people who want to love others. Knowledge is where the Lord deposits his truths that are there all along. People will know more about the Lord and what he knows. As people get hungry to know more and seek knowledge out of love for the Lord and his kingdom plan, he will be found!

Relevance and End Time Survival

What does this have to do with leadership in the days and times ahead? It means that in the times when it does not appear that there is a way out, the Lord will release knowledge of solutions to his people. The book of Proverbs says, "For the turning away of the simple will slay them, and the complacency of fools will destroy them; but *whoever listens to me will dwell safely, and will be secure, without fear of evil*" (Prov. 1:32-33). Those who listen to the Lord will dwell in safety when the world is in chaos. There is nothing for which there is not a solution; there are only solutions that have not yet been found, discovered, or revealed. The Lord is the revealer of hidden knowledge and specific strategies for building, arts, warfare, and management tactics. Even Jesus, while being tempted by Satan, said, "It is written, "Man shall not live by bread alone, *but by every word of God*'" (Luke 4:4). I am not sure that believers usually take that passage to mean revelation knowledge. However, it clearly says by the Word of God, God's people shall live!

The Lord does not change. What he has done in the past, he will do in the present and in the future. The inventions and knowledge that he has given have changed the course of human history and will do so again. The Bible tells that all knowledge will be made known. Luke 12:2 says, "For there is nothing covered that will not be revealed, nor hidden that will not be known." The revelation of knowledge will do humanity no good when in the presence of the Lord, for then all needs will be met. There will be no human need for which there is no solution revealed.

The wisdom that has been released by God on this side of heaven has been for the greater good of humanity. Solomon asked for wisdom for the good of the people of God. The gifts of the Holy Spirit are also for the common good (1 Cor. 12:7). The wisdom and understanding and knowledge that is sought for the common good will be released by the Lord.

Often in history, the people who received the knowledge actively pursued knowledge, but were also in pursuit of God. The pursuit of God is critically important in the quest for knowledge and strategies. God knows the heart. Purity and righteousness, in other words right and proper motives, appeared to be what moved the heart of God many times in Scripture. However, he also often used people across the spectrum, even many who were pagans, but they had a heart for obedience. The Lord God can gift any person he chooses with knowledge and revelation for the greater good. He can bless anyone he chooses and there are usually collateral blessings beyond the one being blessed.

Solomon wrote the words of Proverbs, which seem to give a strategy and a roadmap for solutions and inventions. Solomon said:

> For wisdom is better than rubies; and all the things that may be desired are not to be compared to it. *I wisdom dwell with prudence, and find out knowledge of witty inventions.* The fear of the Lord is to hate evil: pride, and arrogance, and the evil way, and the forward mouth, do I hate. Counsel is mine, and sound wisdom: I am understanding; I have strength. By me kings reign, and princes decree justice. By me princes rule, and nobles, even all the judges of the earth. I love them that love me; *and those that seek me early shall find me.* Riches and honor are with me; yea, durable riches and righteousness. My fruit is better than gold, yea, than fine gold; and my revenue than choice silver. I lead in the way of righteousness, in the midst of the paths of judgment: *That I may cause those that love me to inherit substance; and I will fill their treasures.* (Prov. 8:11-21, KJV)

The conclusion of the matter is this: Scripture confirms that the Lord desires to give knowledge and revelation, but there has to be a willing vessel to receive it. According to the passage in Proverbs, he is looking for those who fear the Lord and hate evil. He will not draw near to pride or a big-mouth response. By this wisdom, kings rule and dispense justice. He is seeking those who love him and who are trusted by him.

Many people I know who are endued with wisdom are early risers. They get up to meet with the Lord and he meets with them. He seems to love the sacrifice of loss of sleep and rewards those who are willing to lay aside personal comfort just to be with him. In fact, the book of Jeremiah confirms that the Lord seeks to teach those who will rise early to be with him: "Therefore thus says the

LORD: ... And they have turned to Me the back, and not the face; *though I taught them, rising up early and teaching them, yet they have not listened to receive instruction"* (Jer. 32:28a, 33). The Lord also said, "But although *I have spoken to you, rising early and speaking,* you did not obey Me. I have also sent to you all My servants the prophets, *rising up early and sending them"* (Jer. 35:14b-15a). It seemed as if the Lord were speaking early, but the people were not rising up early to meet with him and listen. If a person is hungry for more of the Lord, 4 a.m. is a good time to find him. He gives his fruit to those who seek it and his fruit is knowledge. The book of Psalms says, "O God, You are my God; *Early will I seek You;* My soul thirsts for You; My flesh longs for You in a dry and thirsty land Where there is no water" (Ps. 63:1) The thirsty soul will do whatever it takes to find him!

Often those who seek knowledge and wisdom may become wealthy, but actually in those instances wealth is a collateral blessing of seeking God, rather than the result of seeking wealth. The knowledge of God is available to those who seek him; it is available for everyone. Of all the inventions and solutions mentioned in these words, the collateral blessings for each is for the kingdom of God to be advanced and his people blessed! The purpose is not for the person who received the information to find wealth, although that may be a by-product of the revelation. Think about the people mentioned earlier and their discoveries. Overwhelmingly the discoveries were for the greater good of humanity. God does not exist to make us wealthy; humanity exists to glorify God.

This may be a good time to do a "motive self-check." He is looking for vessels. See what needs to be pruned and take a very sharp ax to the root to be made ready to be his pure vessel. There is more information that God has to reveal than can possibly be imagined. As will be discussed later, many different people will get parts of the strategy. No one person can possibly be the receptacle for all the information the Lord wants and needs to flood earth within the days ahead. Ask for it!

Ask, and it will be given to you; seek, and you will find; knock, and it will be opened to you. For everyone who asks receives, and he who seeks finds, and to him who knocks it will be opened. Or what man is there among you who, if his son asks for bread, will give him a stone? Or if he asks for a fish, will he give him a serpent? If you then, being evil, know how to give good gifts to your children, how much more will your Father who is in heaven give good things to those who ask Him! (Matt. 7:7-11)

Chapter 4

The Strategy of Listening Leads to Knowledge

Knowledge is the key to overcoming all obstacles in the kingdom realm. Many people, such as Jehu and Jehoshaphat in the Bible, were given strategies leading to great warfare victories. Strategies come by knowledge from the Lord. People often try to overcome problems or situations alone and they fumble around when they could be operating in the strategies of God. There are strategies in every book of the Bible. However, those strategies are not the only strategies. They are just examples of the kingdom strategies that are available. Too often people want to go to those strategies as the only strategies, but they, like so many things in Scripture, are limited examples of the endless possibilities of God's kingdom strategies. Of course, everything must line up and be in keeping with the words of Scripture. Scripture is the blueprint, not the full house. The book of John says that if the full works of Jesus were written, then the earth could not contain the expanse of information (John 21:25).

People need to think out of the box on solutions to problems and strategies to overcome. We have often sought the pages of Scripture, but there are strategies that line up with the Word and are obedient to God, but they are beyond the Word. Believers will learn much by listening and seeking. The Lord is calling his people to listen more. He wants his people to listen more and seek more. He wants his people to be amazed at the things that he will show for answers and strategies. There is nothing in the Word about drilling for oil, yet sometimes that is the answer. Sometimes people get solutions that are not found in Scripture because the things that the current generation has available were not available when Scripture was written. Many ministries have vans and those vans are used for kingdom purposes, but there is nothing in Scripture about buying a ministry van. People may say, "We know it was God's will for us to buy a van." This is but one example of something that believers do that is a strategy for ministry that is not specifically enumerated in the Word of God. That is a strategy that lines up with the Word but is not in the Word.

Hearing God Speak

Believers have missed many things that will change the world in advancing God's kingdom by not listening to God and hearing his voice. It is necessary and critical that ALL believers have revelation of the spoken word of God along with the guidance of his written Word. God actually treasures people who can both hear his voice and obey his Word. Did you catch that? A person who hears the voice of God and keeps his written covenant is a special blessing to the Lord. This joining of the Spirit and the Word makes the believer a more useful tool than the person could be with just the Spirit or just the Word. Having one part without the other leaves the believer without the full arsenal to be God's kingdom worker and to fight the enemy. The book of Exodus illustrates how important Word and Spirit together are to make God's people kingdom workers who are precious to him: "Now therefore, if you will indeed *obey My voice (Spirit) and keep My covenant (Word)*, then you shall be a special treasure to Me above all people; for all the earth is Mine" (Exod. 19:5, explanatory notes added).

The Lord spoke to me and said, "I want people to have what is available in my kingdom. I see their needs and hurts. I want them to be blessed as I know they can be, *but they have to want it, trust in me, be in faith, and be lined up with the Word.*" This statement breaks down like this:

- People have to want what is available in God's kingdom. They have to be in desperation. This is about intentional seeking. David said there was one thing that he desired and that was to be with the Lord, to see his beauty, and to hear what the Lord would say to him: "One thing I have desired of the LORD, that will I seek: That I may dwell in the house of the LORD All the days of my life, to behold the beauty of the LORD, and to inquire in His temple" (Ps. 27:4). That heartfelt cry was devotion to the Lord above all else.
- People have to trust in the Lord. Hebrews 11:6 says in part, "For he who comes to God must believe that *He Is.*" This is reminiscent of the divine name, "I Am." He is, he was, he always will be. Saying God "Is" is all that is needed. There is no other explanation; he just "Is."
- People have to be in faith. Not only do believers believe that "God Is," people must believe that he can do what he has said he will do. Nothing is impossible with God.
- Finally, people must be lined up with the Word. That means that the teachings are doctrinally sound and do not contain heresy.

These are keys to getting strategy from the kingdom of God. Strategy is the key to overcoming the enemy. Do we not know that the Lord wants the enemy to be overcome? The Lord wants to give the keys, but people are not listening to this. Listening is critical.

Knowledge does not come without hearing, and receiving does not often happen without listening.

The Lord said that people must be taught how to listen. Knowledge does not come without hearing, and receiving does not often happen without listening. People who are distracted do not hear the voice or know the will of the Lord. Many people that I have encountered do not understand the verses in the book of John 10, "I know My sheep, and *am known by My own*"

and "*My sheep hear My voice*, and I know them, and they follow Me" (John 10:14, 27, selections). Most people do not know that they can actually know the voice of the Lord as they know the voices of people they hear every day.

Years after I had been seeking the Lord, I heard the voice of the Lord with the clarity of a conversation, not just an impression. I am not sure it was an audible voice, but it was so real that I turned to see who was speaking to me. It was a day of tremendous break-through for me because it opened up a new realm of communication with the Lord. Before that time, if someone asked me if I heard from the Lord, I probably would have said "Yes," not knowing that there was more. However, there is so much more in terms of information and communication. The Lord wants everyone to have more.

Almost every day, the Lord speaks to me and tells me, "Listen!" (Notice the exclamation mark! That is how he says it... with urgency!) Sometimes he says, "Listen well!" There is so much more he wants to teach his people. He is not telling me to listen so that I will feel bad if I do not. Rather, he is calling me, and everyone, to listen because he knows the possibilities if we do. The kingdom blessings and understanding will be incredible. (That does not to necessarily mean financial blessings, but kingdom blessings.) Listening is key. Listening, when it results in hearing, will bring knowledge.

My husband has been one who always felt that he could not hear the Lord like other people do. One day he wanted to make a gift to a ministry, but he was not sure if it was the right thing to do under the circumstances. Later that evening, he was telling me about the events of the day. He said, "*I heard the Lord say...*" followed by specific instructions. As he was telling me, I instantly caught that the Lord had spoken to him directly, but interestingly enough, he did not catch it.

Mike even told me the specific words that the Lord had spoken to him. Even as he was telling me the story, I knew that he had not heard his own words. I did not mention it that night, but the next morning in my time of seeking, the Lord spoke to me about the matter. Mike did not really get the significance of the way the message was delivered by the Lord: by direct spoken communication. The Lord told me that Mike heard his voice, but it flew by him. Mike got the concept, but he did not have the understanding that he had heard the Lord. Later that day we talked about it and he acknowledged that the Lord had spoken to him, but he had not realized it.

The sheep know and learn to recognize the voice of the shepherd. Shepherds set the stage for the movement of the sheep. They say where and when the sheep move. They provide safety and fend off predators. When the sheep listen, they will not be led astray. I saw a video of a flock of sheep in a field. Some strangers were calling and trying to get the sheep to move or pay attention to them. Three people tried to call the sheep, but the sheep did not even look up from the grass. The people were loud and obnoxious, but the sheep did not even appear to notice them. The shepherd came and called to the sheep. It was amazing to see how the sheep instantly responded to the voice of the shepherd.[11] The sheep started running to the voice of the shepherd, but they would not follow the voice of a stranger. The verses quoted above from John 10 suddenly came to life: the sheep know the voice of their shepherd and they will not follow the voice of a stranger.

That morning the Lord said further, "If Mike will listen, he will have strategies that will bring breakthrough. Do you not know that I want you and Mike to breakthrough? Of course I do, but listening for everything is the key." The Lord cautioned about not leaning on personal and humanistic understanding. The day that Mike began to hear the Lord was a banner day for him, too. It was like when I began to hear the voice of the Lord the day I turned to see who was speaking to me. It changed my life and my communication with the Lord! When people listen, the Lord will show the way and things will be easy. People need to call on the Lord rather than first picking up the phone to call a friend. Ask the Lord first and he will give the desires of his heart. He will lead just as a shepherd leads the flock.

---

[11] https://youtu.be/e45dVgWgV64, Accessed May 12, 2017.

Hearing in the Midst of Distractions

The Lord has been teaching me to cultivate hearing in the midst of distractions. It will be critical in the days ahead. Every person, no matter how mature in the faith, can grow to levels about which have not even yet been dreamed. I prayed, "Lord open the fire hydrant of understanding and hearing... No, open Victoria Falls, the largest waterfall in the world! Open up whatever I can handle." The Lord answered me and said, "Victoria falls could roll for a million years with information, and you would not have scratched the surface."

People who are starving to know more will cultivate hearing him in the midst of distractions. The Lord needs our spiritual ears tuned in to hear him. People do not hear with their ears in the kingdom realm; they hear with their minds. There will be more about that in a chapter on the deaf and dumb spirit and the limitation on hearing with the mind. There may be times when our lives depend on hearing the Lord when all around are losing their heads. It is important to seek knowledge and overcome distractions because the enemy will always seek to distract with whatever he can.

My husband and I, along with two other couples, felt led into prayer for six days. The pastor had a Holy Spirit leading that the Lord had called forth a time of special seeking. The Lord was calling this time of prayer and fasting to seek his face. We did not ask for anything; we merely were seeking the Lord's will and glorifying him to the best of our ability. The pastor called a gathering on Saturday to discuss what the Lord was calling us to do before we began the prayer assemblies on Monday.

As I left the meeting on Saturday, I knew in my heart that I was going to have to be dedicated and intentional about getting to the prayer meeting and seeking to hear the Lord. I knew in my heart that the enemy would do whatever he could to stop the call of the Lord to prayer and listening. I fully understood that this time of special seeking was ordained by God, and not just another called meeting. The first night, one person hit a deer on her way to prayer and did severe damage to her car. She went home and never made it to prayer during all the days of the prayer meeting. Other people had deer run out in front of them and owls swooping at their cars. There were other distractions to divert and dissuade.

The second afternoon, about three hours before the time of prayer, my daughter sent a text and said that she was in the emergency room at the hospital with her heart. My daughter had some previous incidents with cardiac issues and was under the care of a cardiologist. I previously felt that we had come to the end of the issue, both physically and spiritually. I knew the timing of this was a spiritual attack to keep me from going to prayer. Of course I rushed to the hospital although I had peace that the Lord had the situation in control. My son-in-law was working out of town. When he arrived a little later, I asked him if he wanted to get something to eat because I had to leave at a certain time. My daughter begged me not to go and to stay with her. I told her, "The United States has a policy that it does not negotiate with terrorists. This is nothing more than a terrorist attack, and I refuse to negotiate. If the enemy thinks that he can stop me by attacking you, there will be no end to the attacks that you will experience. Wild horses could not keep me away from that prayer meeting." I asked her if she understood and she said that she did.

When it came time for me to depart, she cried and begged me not to go. I knew in my heart that it was the best thing for her even if she could not see it in that moment. We overcame that attack. I went to prayer and she was released from the hospital while I was in the prayer meeting. She did not have anymore incidents, and I firmly believe that she will not have anymore either. One more thing: When I arrived at the hospital, I could not go into the emergency room right away. I went to the waiting room and prayed for every person there. When the enemy goes after your camp, go after his.

The Lord was with us. I pray that people will understand that I was being a better mother, not a worse one, by going to prayer and not letting the demonic attack stop me. In the end, my daughter was at complete peace. I pray that she also learned a valuable lesson that will benefit her when her own children are attacked to stop her from following God's will someday. Love the Lord your God with all your heart, soul, mind, and strength, and your neighbor as yourself. I believed that as I dedicated myself to serve the Lord, that he would take care of my daughter in ways that I could not even begin to imagine. The Lord wants to show great strategies and teach all that we will need to know. One of the strategies that he taught me was carrying on in the midst of many distractions. Cultivate hearing.

It was hard on my daughter that I left, but it was hard on me too. The strength to do it was born out of peace and faith and that the Lord had shown me on that Saturday night at the initial meeting that I was going to have to be "set" to let nothing stop me. We did not have any more distractions during the remainder of the time dedicated to prayer. I attribute that to the fact that we overcame a serious attack and were victorious in the Lord. The Lord is going to teach this strategy well so that we will be able to hear him in the midst of greater chaos than this situation. To overcome, believers must be able to hear him when the world is losing its head, literally and figuratively.

Partial Strategy Released to Many

One morning, I was up early seeking the Lord and listening. It had been a particularly prolific journaling day. I had journaled about five single-spaced pages of conversation with the Lord. At the very end, the Lord dropped a kernel of truth into my spirit. He simply said,

> Laura, listen now about strategy: The end-time strategy will be intense. Several people will have the strategy. The parts of it will fit together like the pieces of a puzzle. If there is not unity, the strategy will not be fully revealed! Partial or half information is often worse than no information.

When the Lord started speaking and said, "Several people will have the strategy," I instantly interpreted that to mean that he would give many people the whole strategy. He quickly corrected me and I knew that several people would have only parts of the strategy. If the people are not in one accord, the body of Christ will not get the full strategy of God. Partial strategy in wartime is very dangerous. Unity in the body will be critical.

Think of one piece of a 1,000-piece jigsaw puzzle. It shows almost nothing of what the full picture will look like when it is not joined with all the other pieces. The full picture will not be revealed until all of the pieces are in their right and proper place. The first thing that most people do is dump out all the puzzle pieces on a table and turn them right-side up. The pieces are all there, but until they are in their right and proper place, there is still very little information that can be gleaned about the full picture of the puzzle. If one is not looking at the box top with the full picture, but only at the puzzle pieces scattered on a table, there is not much that can be gained by looking at the chaos of the scattered pieces.

The metaphor of the puzzle provides a message for the Church and for apostolic leaders: The parts of the body of Christ must be in their right and proper place in order to fulfill God's plan and purposes. Everything God has created is done in order. The formation of the body of Christ is no different. Apostolic leaders are called to help people find their right place. The knowledge and strategy that each person has will not be useful until there is kingdom order in the overall whole picture. The massive amount of knowledge will be overwhelming if there is disunity or disorder. The body of Christ must be in order, like a well-trained army, to be fully effective to do what the Lord wants and needs it to do as the times intensify.

Knowledge will increase and it will even be frightful because it will be more than people can take in, and that is why some people will get parts of the strategy and some will get other parts of the strategy. The flow of information from the throne room of God to the earth will be immense. That is one strategy of the kingdom of God to overcome and keep the enemy so busy that the information gets through to vessels ready and willing to receive it. Preparation of the vessels will be necessary: "Therefore if anyone cleanses himself from the latter, he will be a vessel for honor, sanctified and useful for the Master, prepared for every good work" (2 Tim. 2:21). There will be a bombardment of knowledge and understanding that is released from heaven and the enemy will not be able to stop or delay it all. Much of it will get through simply because of the vastness of what is released from the heavenly realm. The vessels must be ready to receive it by being cleansed from all unrighteousness.

Daniel set himself to seek the Lord in Daniel 10. The Lord heard the prayer on the first day and sent the answer. However, it took Daniel twenty-one days to get his message because of the warfare in the heavenly realm. The Lord may release information, but if it is delayed by demons and demonic principalities in the second heavenly realm, it slows down the process of God's plans, which is what Satan wants to do. I believe that one of God's strategies in the end will be to release a flood of information. For the enemy, it will be like putting fingers in the holes of a dam. Eventually the pressure of the water coming through will cause larger and larger breaches in the dam until there is complete dam failure so that the knowledge can flow. Remember the book of Habakkuk says, "For the earth will be filled with the knowledge of the glory of the LORD, As the waters cover the sea" (Hab. 2:14). This is reminiscent of the flood of Genesis. That is a lot of knowledge! It will come in a great release from the Lord.

The increase of knowledge will also baffle the enemy's camp. This is just like when Gideon culled his army to 300 men, but the enemy's camp was thrown into confusion by the broken vessels and trumpets and lights (Judg. 7:7). Think what that means in the Spirit realm. The broken vessels represent people yielded and broken before the Lord, allowing the sounds of heaven and the glory of God to come through. The trumpets represent the voice of God, which caused confusion in the opposing army. The same was true as Jesus walked on the earth; many mistook the sound of the voice of the Father for thunder (John 12:29).

Many will get parts of the strategy, but people will have to work together in unity to see God's purpose fulfilled. Here is more evidence of that release of strategy: A man of Africa had a dream in 2011 about the deaf and dumb spirit. For six years, he had no interpretation of the dream but knew somehow that he had to minister to people who were burdened by the deaf and dumb spirit. He stumbled onto a video teaching on my webpage about that particular spirit. The Lord gave me a very similar vision to his and then helped me unpack it in the Scripture. He wrote these messages about how the Lord had used the similar dreams and visions to bring understanding. It is like the situation between Daniel and Nebuchadnezzar when they had similar dreams (Dan. 2:24). One with knowledge from God could interpret it for the other who did not have the knowledge from God. The African man had a dream he could not understand, and I had a similar vision and the Lord gave the interpretation of it. The man wrote:

> Hello, thank you so much for sharing the revelation that you have from the Lord with us concerning the deaf and dumb spirit. Your teaching has opened my spiritual eyes to see my calling clearly.

Later he also shared:

> My mission is to evangelize and teach deaf people so that they may be healed and serve the Lord. The Lord has put this passion in my heart. I really knew (little) about the deaf and dumb spirit but I got a revelation yesterday when I was watching your teaching on YouTube. In 2011, I saw in a dream a man with a cap on his head and a stethoscope on his neck. I didn't understand the vision since 2011, but yesterday my eyes were opened. When I think about the passion that I have, that I was not able to understand, and the dream that I had in 2011, I come to the conclusion that I have found God's purpose for my life.

In the days ahead, unity in the body will be critical because, as in these examples, different people will have different parts of the strategy. If the body of Christ does not work together, it will be unable to know and recognize the full plan of God. Spiritual hearing will be critical to receive and understand the revelation of God.

Chapter 5

God's Time is Often Bamboo Time

Late one spring I was working in my flowers. For many weeks I had been pruning, planting, and fertilizing the garden. I had also bought some bare-root flowers and planted them. Every day or two I checked to see if any growth was peeking out from the soil. After many days, I finally began to see one or two little shoots coming up. I continued to watch the plants for many days. Even in the midst of an absolutely beautiful and favorable spring growing season, the plants were just barely out of the ground. Days and weeks passed without much change. Things were moving slowly in the garden. The Lord spoke to me and said, "You have fed the plants and expect to see marvelous and magnificent growth. You think things are creeping at a snail's pace. You will go out one day and see exponential growth. You will be amazed at the level of growth overnight. That is how my kingdom will grow on the earth."

There are times in life and in ministry that we may be doing all the right things but do not see much happening. One day, the plant will break the surface of the ground, and the growth will be amazing. The Lord further said, "Seeing the garden develop slowly is a reflection of the kingdom growth in your life and the lives of those around you. You think that not much is happening. One day - BOOM! - and there is explosive growth." The encouragement came to illustrate that even though there was no visible growth that

I could see, there was growth activity going on that was not visible. There was growth under the ground.

The seemingly invisible kingdom expansion can be described in gardening terms. The roots of the plants were being developed to sustain the growth above the ground. If the roots were sub-standard, the plants could not be sustained when they sprouted. The roots are the foundation of the plants. The roots must be sure and ready to handle the growth that would soon come. The roots below the ground carry the beautiful growth that is seen above the ground. If the above-ground plant developed too fast, the plant would be weak and would not be sustained in wind or drought or other times of stress and hardship. The bare-root plants that I planted, upon maturity, would be about four or five feet tall. Without an adequate root system, they would blow over at the first puff of wind.

I told my apostolic pastor and spiritual mentor what the Lord told me, especially about the roots developing while nothing appeared to be happening. He referred to the apparent delay as *bamboo time*. The apparent delay is not really delay at all, but rather activity-under-the-ground time. The phrase *bamboo time* comes from the observation of the bamboo plant, which is actually considered a grass. Bamboo responds well to good conditions, but even so, there may be little or no outward above-ground growth for years. In the first few years, there is little visible sign of activity. Finally, when the time is right, something almost miraculous happens. It is almost like watching a real-life version of Jack's beanstalk grow up overnight. The plant springs forth from God's ordained plan from nothingness into a giant botanical specimen. The plant was not actually dormant during that lengthy time while nothing appeared to be happening. Even though the growth was not visible, the plant was growing underground. It was growing and developing a root system strong enough to support its potential for rapid above-ground growth. It was necessary that the plant have a firm foundation so that the upward growth was secure.

There are times that seem sleepy and those in the body of Christ feel that nothing is happening. People are working, doing, praying, fasting, seeking, discerning, and worshiping, but there is no outward sign that the Lord is hearing or that prayers are getting through. At times it may even seem worse when there are promises from the Lord or prophetic words have been given that line up with the call of the Lord. During those times, people may begin to wonder if they missed the opportunity or question even if there was a call of the Lord. People are praying and waiting and believing with expectation, sometimes for years, and it seems as if nothing is happening. Finally, *if people do not give up*, those words will mature and ripen into full manifestation. Galatians says, "And let us not grow weary while doing good, for in due season *we shall reap if we do not lose heart*" (Gal. 6:9). Sometimes the Lord works in bamboo time.

I saw a twenty-four-hour time-lapse video of bamboo as it sprang forth from the earth after the long delay of root time.[12] Under right and proper conditions, the bamboo can grow almost five feet in a single day. Some bamboo grows eighty to one hundred feet in just six weeks. The twenty-four-hour video showed the plant breaking forth from the earth and sprouting up to be many feet tall. It was amazing and actually even somewhat bizarre to watch. It did not seem natural to see the remarkable growth in such a short period.

I started thinking about hidden things ... roots, insulation, subfloor, buried or planted seeds, blood, internal organs, the floor of the ocean, the vastness of the universe, and so many other things that we know are there, but cannot see. Hidden things are the sub-floor structures or support of everything that is visible. Often, what is hidden is the support for that which is exposed. The book of Hebrews says, "By faith we understand that the worlds were framed by the Word of God, *so that the things which are seen were not made of things which are visible*" (Heb. 11:3). The Greek word for the phrase *the things which are seen* is *blepō*. It is a verb which means "to look at, behold, perceive, regard, see, sight, or take heed." The Greek word for the phrase *the things which are visible* is *phainō* and it means "to lighten, that is, show, be seen, shine." I would paraphrase Hebrews 11:3 to say, "The things that we behold and see are not made of the things that come to light or are seen." Similarly, 2 Corinthians says,

---

[12] https://youtu.be/FfDOMwFX5Hg Accessed May 18, 2017.

> Therefore, we do not lose heart. Even though our
> outward man is perishing, yet the inward man is
> being renewed day by day. For our light affliction,
> which is but for a moment, is working for us a far
> more exceeding and eternal weight of glory, *while*
> *we do not look at the things which are seen, but at*
> *the things which are not seen. For the things which*
> *are seen are temporary, but the things which are not*
> *seen are eternal.* (2 Cor. 4:16-18)

The things seen by humanity in the natural realm are a poor reflection of what is not seen, those things that are in the heavenly realm but are not visible. Peering into the realm of God's kingdom is about peering into the realm that has not yet come to light. The realm of the kingdom of God is there all the time, but unnoticed by most in the natural realm. The Lord said about this discussion, "I will pull back the curtain for you so that you can see and experience the kingdom realm. The amount and significance is up to you."

There Are No "Suddenly Moments" in God's Plan

The bamboo was hidden, and then in what appeared to be a *suddenly moment*, it broke through the ground. Occasionally, there are suddenly moments on the pages of Scripture and in the lives of people. The real question is then, "Who are they 'sudden' for?" In actuality, those moments are not suddenly moments at all. They may be perceived as being sudden from the human perspective, but those moments are not a surprise to the Lord. They may be the culmination of years of kingdom planning and are the fulfillment of things that God has been moving in all along. God may see a course of action unfolding and be aware of it, but he is never caught off guard.

In the time of root growth, the bamboo was hidden. It appeared to come forth suddenly, but it was not sudden. The above-ground growth was well calculated to come forth at just the right time. Suddenly is a concept that is often misunderstood in the natural as it applies to the kingdom of God. There are no suddenly moments in the kingdom of God because with him everything is known from the foundation of the world. How can something be a surprise or an unexpected event for the One who is all-knowing? Things may seem to be sudden to the children of the earth, but there are no sudden moments in God's kingdom. The Lord sees all from the beginning.

Daniel 10 illustrates what happens in the heavenly realm when prayers are prayed on the earth. As briefly discussed in the last chapter, Daniel prayed for twenty-one days before the prayer was answered. From Daniel's perspective there was a suddenly moment: "I lifted my eyes and looked, and *behold*, a certain man clothed in linen, whose waist was girded with gold of Uphaz!" (Dan. 10:5). The word *behold* in Scripture has the suggestion of surprise. Daniel was surprised. However, from the perspective of the heavenly realm, it was well known what was happening to bring Daniel the message. The Daniel passage continues, "Then he said to me, "Do not fear, Daniel, *for from the first day that you set your heart to understand*, and to humble yourself before your God, *your words were heard; and I have come because of your words*" (Dan. 10:12). There was no surprise in heaven. As long as Daniel continued to pray, and did not lose heart, he should have been in anticipation for the answer. With continued prayer, there should be nothing but expectation. If Daniel was waiting, knowing, and seeking with a whole heart, the answer should have been anticipated.

Actually, the "suddenly" response shows a lack of faith in some ways. Believers should consider the possibility of not responding to "suddenly" moments, but responding to the "expectation" that God will act on our behalf when we pray in keeping with his will. The book of 1 John says, "Now this is the confidence that we have in Him, that if we ask anything according to His will, He hears us. And if we know that He hears us, whatever we ask, we know that we have the petitions that we have asked of Him" (1 John 5:14-15). In all honesty (and giving Daniel a break), expectation

The "suddenly" response shows a lack of faith in some ways. Believers should respond to the expectation that God will act when we pray in keeping with his will.

is more challenging the longer the time in prayer without the answer. There can be no surprise in the heavenly realm with the Lord and those who know the mind of Christ because God is omniscient, or all-knowing. The response time for Daniel was long, but the message was on the way from the beginning.

Many believers have been in bamboo time for a long while. Some even much, much longer than Daniel. However, there is no surprise to the kingdom realm that the shoot is about to spring forth from the ground. What is happening under the ground is growth activity. Simply because people cannot see, that does not mean that nothing is happening. Believers walk by faith and not by sight (2 Cor. 5:7). This is also where listening to God is very beneficial. In those times of delay, the Lord will give encouragement if people will pause to listen. I can testify from first-hand experience that God has encouraged my husband and me during times of long delays, during bamboo time. God will give the strategy of knowledge, when people seek it, even if the strategy is simply to wait.

Faith is necessary during bamboo time: "Now faith is the substance of things hoped for (the bamboo stalk that is expected to grow up), the evidence of things not seen (the below-ground root growth)" (Heb. 11:1). Faith is grabbing hold of what is happening in the unseen kingdom realm. Bamboo time is knowing that things are happening in the heavenly realm, even when there is nothing happening in the natural realm. That is the "evidence of things not seen." Things are always happening when people are praying according to God's will, such as in the Daniel passage above. If prayers are offered in keeping with God's will, why would he not be working? Praying for the will of the Lord to be accomplished is always the right way to pray (See 1 John 5:14-15, referenced above). Hebrews 11 is known as the *faith chapter*. In the faith chapter, there is not one mention of the words, "immediately," "suddenly," or "behold." By way of another example, Noah was not surprised that the rain came and that the floods of the deep opened up. He expected it.

God is never surprised. Surprise suggests uncertainty about what is coming. God is never in ambiguity about what is going to happen. God has to understand surprise because people have that response and emotion. In that regard, we may even experience something that God does not experience. If we are Christlike and have the mind of Christ, then we should not be surprised when we see the answers arrive in response to prayers prayed in the will of God. God reveals through the revelation of the Holy Spirit:

> But God has revealed them to us through His Spirit. For the Spirit searches all things, yes, the deep things of God. For what man knows the things of a man except the spirit of the man which is in him? Even so no one knows the things of God except the Spirit of God. Now we have received, not the spirit of the world, but the Spirit who is from God, that we might know the things that have been freely given to us by God. These things we also speak, not in words which man's wisdom teaches but which the Holy Spirit teaches, comparing spiritual things with spiritual. But the natural man does not receive the things of the Spirit of God, for they are foolishness to him; nor can he know them, because they are spiritually discerned. But he who is spiritual judges all things, yet he himself is rightly judged by no one. For "Who has known the mind of the Lord that he may instruct him?" *But we have the mind of Christ.* (1 Cor. 2:10-16)

The recognized historical Bible commentator, Matthew Henry, says, "(Jesus Christ) is God, and the principal messenger and prophet of God. And the apostles were empowered by his Spirit to make known his mind to us. And in the holy Scriptures the mind of Christ, and the mind of God in Christ, are fully revealed to us. *Observe, it is the great privilege of Christians that they have the mind of Christ revealed to them by his Spirit.*"[13] Knowing what God knows means having the mind of Christ. If God is never surprised, then believers will not be surprised either. Following that to the

---

[13] http://www.biblestudytools.com/commentaries/matthew-henry-complete/1-corinthians/2.html Accessed June 3, 2017.

logical conclusion, when believers are in communion with the Spirit of God, they have the mind of Christ. The Spirit of God knows everything, so believers will know what he knows and chooses to reveal to us. Believers who are in communion with the Holy Spirit will not be caught off guard.

God never does anything that he does not reveal first to his prophets. There should never be an adverse suddenly moment that takes believers by surprise! "Surely the Lord God does nothing, unless He reveals His secret to His servants the prophets" (Amos 3:7). In a perfect world, there should be no more suddenly moments if the people are listening and receiving the revelation and prophetic utterance from God. He is not a God of surprise, and if his people have his mind, the people are not a people of surprise either. God's people have something to seek from the Lord and that is knowing what he knows so that we are not surprised. (There will be more on surprise later in a chapter on warfare strategies. The goal is not to be surprised, while surprising our enemy.)

Thinking back to the bare-roots planted in my garden, I was walking in expectation. Looking every day or two to see if the plants had sprouted did not lend itself to the response of surprise. There was great suspense and anticipation. However, one element of surprise and, in fact, the only element of surprise that believers should allow is the element of surprise in the magnitude of God's response to our prayers. In other words, we are not surprised that God answers, but we are blown away by the magnitude of his response. Dream big of a big God. He is not a pauper and he does not answer in the way of a pauper. But even so, knowing that God is who he is: Is surprise ever a proper response to him? Thanksgiving, praise, and worship may be better responses.

What is the proper response to the overwhelming outflow of God's blessing and favor? Jehoshaphat praised God all the way back to Jerusalem in 2 Chronicles 20. Other people throughout Scripture went away praising God! Surprise is a brief mental and physiological state, a startle response experienced by people as the result of an unexpected event. Familiarity reduces surprise. Familiarity with God reduces surprise at his actions. Knowing God reduces the likelihood of unexpected suddenly moments.

There really should not be surprised moments, only moments of fulfilled expectation. Fulfilled expectation is a moment of fulfillment of understanding. Surprise can only come where there is no understanding. As believers seek to grow in knowledge and understanding, there will be less and less surprise. The greater the level of relationship, the greater the opportunity for receiving fulfilled expectations.

Chapter 6

Minor Corrections Leading to Massive Expansions

"Don't do it that way. Do it this way." Most people have heard those statements sometime during their lives, whether from a chemistry professor teaching how to do an experiment, or from a mother showing how to crack an egg. People often learn from others who know more or who have learned from their own past mistakes. Often in life, a minor course correction is necessary. That is true as humanity seeks to have the doors opened to the kingdom of God. Sometimes the doors of knowledge remain closed because there are things in a person's life that demand to be changed or corrected or purified before he or she can walk into the fullness of God's plan. Doing things Jesus' way changes the outcome. A person can plod and prod along, being off course just a bit, and miss the mark of where God wants him or her to be.

My husband had been handling our tithing in a way that seemed to make since to take advantage of the tax laws. My husband became aware of a teaching on tithes, offerings, and extravagant offerings by Robert Morris.[14] He loved a twenty-minute segment of the video and showed many people in his law office. He showed

---

[14] https://www.youtube.com/watch?v=ZlcVo8yOoBw Accessed April 27, 2016. This video is 3:08 in length. The segment that touched my husband began at 2:50 to the end.

colleagues and friends. He showed ministry partners. Basically, he showed anyone who would watch the video clip with him. He was blown away with the teaching about handling money God's way and the testimonies that followed.

There was one small problem. We were not adhering to the teaching in the way that we were giving our tithes and offerings. Being a good and dutiful wife, I shared that little fact with my husband. He paused and said (mark this down ☺), "You are right." After a short discussion he said, "We will change at the first of the month." The beginning of the month was about three weeks away. I said to him, "Why would we want to be in rebellion for another three weeks?" He changed our policies immediately.

The next day several blessings and instances of God's favor began to emerge. We could instantly see God's blessing on the decision that we had just made. For a long while I had felt and understood that we needed to make some minor corrections in our thinking and in some of our practices. I believe that was God leading me to a kingdom strategy. I just sensed that minor corrections would lead to massive expansions. The next day, doors began to open for business opportunities to be fulfilled. One of our employees, who seemed to be an unlikely prophetic voice, started hearing the Lord speak. He gave us prophetic words from the Lord that we discerned to be true and accurate. The voice of prophecy gave directions for financial blessings that would bless our business, and in turn, expand our giving. Also, the next day the cell phone company *called us* and said they wanted to change our business plan to save us several hundred dollars per month. How often does it happen that someone takes the initiative to call to take money out of his or her pocket to save money in your pocket? That is God's favor, folks.

I understood what I was seeing take place. There had been minor changes that were leading to major blessings. It made me realize that there are multitudes of Christians all over the world that may need to make some minor changes so that there can be major expansions. They think they are in God's will, but they may be off just enough that the Lord cannot or will not bless them. The most challenging and tricky deception of Satan is the one that is the closest to the truth. If he can tinker with a person's understanding of the Word just enough that it is wrong, then he has won the battle. The plan is that people will be in a position to hear God, know him, know his revelations, and walk in his strategies. People who are off even a small amount may not hear and be in a position to receive the revelations of God. A minor correction may be needed to walk in God's strategies.

Think about the temptations of Jesus. Satan used the word of God to tempt Jesus. He is a pretty bold character to tempt the Word with the Word! However, Satan tweaked the word that he gave just enough so that it would not be a truthful rendition of the Word of God (Luke 4). It was off just enough to be false. That fact alone should let us know how damaging even subtle changes to the understanding of the Word of God can be.

The most challenging and tricky deception of Satan is the one that is the closest to the truth. If he can tinker with a person's understanding of the Word just enough that it is wrong, then he has won the battle.

Sometimes tweaking natural actions may lead to major manifestations of kingdom reality. One biblical example of a minor correction which led to a major expansion came from Peter and the others putting the net on the other side of the boat. They fished *their way* all night, but one minor correction led to major kingdom revelation. In the morning, Jesus was on the shore while they fished. The book of John reports, "Jesus said to them, 'Children, have you any food?' They answered Him, 'No.' And He said to them, 'Cast the net on the right side of the boat, and you will find some.' So they cast, and now they were not able to draw it in because of the multitude of fish" (John 21:5-6).

What was the actual span of the boat? How much distance between the two sides? The boats of that era were small, so ten feet perhaps? The Sea of Galilee is a good-sized body of water. Even so, by "sea" standards, it is little more than a puddle, with dimensions of about seven miles by fourteen miles. It is easy to stand on one shore of the Sea of Galilee and see the other shore. In the natural, a few feet should not make a difference between nothing and a vast harvest. But this was not a natural event; it was a supernatural event. The difference in harvest was the difference in the disciples doing it *their way* versus doing it *Jesus' way* and according to his revelation.

The example of Peter throwing the net on the right side is a wonderful biblical example of how a minor correction may lead to a major expansion or harvest. When believers are aligned with the will and Word of the Lord, supernatural things will begin to happen. This is about being fully aligned with God's way and not doing things our way. This was a minor course correction. For purposes of the strategy of knowledge, it is really about hearing what the Lord is saying and doing it. Hearing the Lord leads to a change from the way that a person is doing things into the way that Jesus wants things done. Often the minor correction of doing things his way will lead to his kingdom manifestation.

The Infinity of Crescendo

If minor corrections are not made, the continuing error just takes a person further away from the Lord's plan. The Lord began speaking about a crescendo mark in music as a metaphor of how a minor correction may change a person's future. A crescendo mark is a symbol on a musical score indicating a gradual, steady increase in loudness or force of sound. The actual crescendo symbol is a great representation and example of what happens when believers are off course, even the slightest amount. The crescendo mark consists of two lines that are joined on the left side but gradually separate and go farther apart over the course of the symbol. It may be easy to imagine an elongated "V" turned on its side. If the lines of the crescendo continue into eternity, the lines would grow further apart with each measure of distance. If they continued on the trajectory, they would never meet and always continue to grow further apart. That is how it is when a person is on the path away from the will of God. The further a person travels on the wrong course, the further he or she is from God's will.

Another example comes to mind is a scene from the drama played out in the movie *Apollo 13*. The space mission was to land on the moon. However, before the three astronauts ever made it to the moon, there was a serious malfunction of the spacecraft. In one scene, the badly injured spacecraft was drifting off course. They needed to be on a trajectory to a very narrow window to re-enter the earth's atmosphere and get home. In other words, by example they may have been on one line of the crescendo mark, but they needed to be on the other line. The further they went in the wrong direction the greater the distance they were from their goal of getting home to earth.

They were off course. If the distance to be traveled was a short distance, being off course is not as much of a problem as if the distance is great. However, when there is a span of thousands upon thousands of miles to travel, even one-degree of error can make the difference in success or failure. The Apollo 13 astronauts had a window of about 4 degrees. They needed to make a course correction so they would not just be lost in space drifting for all time, having missed the narrow window of opportunity to get back to earth. They turned on the engines to fire up their space module. At least in the movie version of the events, the module was jumping all over the place as they were trying to change their course so that they could get lined up to encounter the earth's atmosphere. In the end, the astronauts made it home. They made a course correction and managed to hit the target.

The whole point of all of this is that when Christians are off course even a little bit in their understanding, it may be enough to keep them from reaching the goal of walking fully in God's will. It may be enough to keep believers from hearing the plans and strategies of God. This is a season for minor change which will lead to major expansions. It is a time for mid-course corrections. Listening and hearing the Lord, and then doing what he says, gives believers the knowledge to be in his strategy and will.

Failure to Make a Mid-Course Correction

If believers will just look, it is obvious how a failure to make a correction is a decision that will take them further from the kingdom of God. The rich young ruler refused to make a midcourse correction. He asked Jesus what he needed to do. When Jesus told him, he went away dejected. He would not make the changes in his life to place himself in the will of God. He was presented with an opportunity to give up very little, even though vast by worldly standards, to have everything by kingdom standards (Mark 10:17-22). His failure to change took him away from God's kingdom rather than toward it.

On the other hand, Peter made a midcourse correction by the sea. He caught an abundance of fish after catching nothing all night. Look what happened in both instances. Jesus was there giving directions to those who would listen. The one who listened changed course, but the other one did not. Adjustments bring things into alignment. When we are out of line with the kingdom plan, we are in the wrong place with God.

Take a look at Joseph in the Old Testament (Gen. 37, et. seq.). He was languishing in prison. Fortuitously, two of pharaoh's officials had dreams that needed to be interpreted. The officials said to Joseph, "We each have had a dream, and there is no interpreter of it." So Joseph said to them, "*Do not interpretations belong to God? Tell them to me*, please" (Gen. 40:8). Joseph did mention in passing that interpretations belong to God, but look what happened after that:

> And Joseph said to (the cupbearer), "*This is the interpretation of it*: The three branches are three days. Now within three days Pharaoh will lift up your head and restore you to your place, and you will put Pharaoh's cup in his hand according to the former manner, when you were his butler. But *remember me* when it is well with you, and please *show kindness to me*; make *mention of me* to Pharaoh, and *get me out of this house.* ... So Joseph answered (the baker) and said, "*This is the interpretation of it.* ... (Gen. 40:12-14, 18)

Joseph never gave glory to God when the dreams were interpreted for the baker and cupbearer. He never thanked the Lord or glorified him for the kingdom knowledge and revelation. He never mentioned the Lord again. However, as events played out, he had another opportunity. The Pharaoh had dreams that could not be interpreted, and the cupbearer remembered Joseph:

> Now there was a *young Hebrew man* with us there, a servant of the captain of the guard. And we told him, and *he interpreted* our dreams for us; to each man *he interpreted* according to his own dream. And it came to pass, just as *he interpreted for us*, so it happened. He restored me to my office, and he hanged him." (Gen. 41:12-13)

The cupbearer never mentioned that God was the interpreter of dreams. Could it be that because Joseph cast the spotlight on himself, the official did not know to give glory to God? See what the Pharaoh said to Joseph, "I have had a dream, and there is no one who can interpret it. But *I have heard it said of you* that *you* can understand a dream, to interpret it" (Gen. 41:15). The Egyptians placed all of their faith in Joseph in these encounters, never acknowledging God at all.

When Joseph was called forth from the prison, his attitude had changed. This time Joseph placed all attention on the Lord from the first words he uttered. Joseph answered Pharaoh, saying,

> "*It is not in me*; *God will give* Pharaoh an answer of peace." ... Then Joseph said to Pharaoh, "The dreams of Pharaoh are one; *God has shown* Pharaoh what He is about to do." ... "And the dream was repeated to Pharaoh twice because the thing is *established by God, and God will shortly bring it to pass*." (Gen. 41:16, 25, 33)

In the first encounter, it appeared that Joseph engaged in self-advancement, or at least, did not give glory to God. Did a course correction take place in the middle while Joseph was still languishing in the prison for another two years? Was Joseph in the flesh when he interpreted the first two dreams? Did he want to draw more attention to himself than he did to God? Was he trying to orchestrate his own release from bondage rather than relying on the Lord? Was His wilderness time increased because he needed a minor correction?

Joseph actually did the same thing both times; he interpreted dreams by the will of God. But one time, God received all the glory and the other time the Lord did not receive glory. When the cup-bearer remembered the earlier situation, he said nothing about God. The entirety of his conversation with Pharaoh was all about Joseph. In the second situation when Joseph talked to Pharaoh, Joseph's response was vastly different than the first time.

When Joseph came before the Pharaoh, the first thing he did was give God the glory for the revelation. He could only interpret the dreams by the power of the Spirit of God, but that was never heard of until he mentioned God to Pharaoh at least four times. That time Pharaoh even acknowledged the work of God in Joseph's life because everything that Joseph said pointed to God. Pharaoh said to his servants, "Can we find such a one as this, *a man in whom is the Spirit of God?*" (Gen 41:38). That time Joseph glorified God, but the first time he did not.

Joseph made a minor course correction along the way. God will bless humility, but he will resist pride. As Joseph sat in prison for another two years, he may have had a long time to think about his conversations with the baker and cupbearer. By the time he came before Pharaoh, he could not wait to glorify God!

What a person does on earth will establish his or her eternity. Not just the place of eternity, but the position. As a believer decides to yield to the Lord in all areas, making minor corrections of things that are out of order, he or she will move into alignment with God. God wants to bless his people, but sometimes they are not in a position to be blessed by him because situations or attitudes are out of order. A person may need to make minor corrections that will lead to major blessings. As a person learns to listen and seek him, the Lord will give the knowledge and strategy to get in alignment so that the believer can both be effective for his kingdom and to be blessed by him.

Chapter 7

Knowledge of Communication

Communication is vital in any offensive. Knowledge will be important in the end. Knowledge will increase. We have not seen anything yet compared to the knowledge explosion that is sure to come. Even now many things are obsolete by the time they make it to market, but I am not talking about that. I am talking about mental understanding and even mental communications. Testimonies abound from people who have visited the heavenly realm who have experienced communication with no words. For example, when angels are present, there may be thought exchange with no spoken form of communication. It amounts to a spiritual exchange of information without the necessity of engaging in speech or hearing, as in the natural realm. That will begin to happen more and more as time goes on. The enemy has already tried to apprehend this concept by demonic communication such as clairvoyance, extrasensory perception, telepathy, mind reading, or psychic readings, etc. What I am referring to is communication by means of the Spirit of God. The Holy Spirit will communicate to two or more people things that are strategic for the people to know to fulfill God's plans. It is not the people doing it; it is the Holy Spirit providing the same or similar communication to different people.

My friend and I had almost the exact dream one day apart. My dream was staged in the ocean and her dream was set in a pond, but other than that, the dreams were basically the same dream. I woke up and urgently wrote down my dream. A day or two later, when she started telling me her dream, I opened my computer and read my dream to her. We had not communicated about the dreams until that moment.

I always want to confirm that all such occurrences are supported by similar biblical occurrences. I prayed and asked the Lord to show me that this unusual event of two friends having the same dream was supported by the Bible. The Lord instantly reminded me of the biblical dream that Daniel interpreted for Nebuchadnezzar in Daniel 2. The Holy Spirit gave the dream to two people at different times. Both people knew the content of the dream, but they were not operating in some form of unholy soul tie or telepathy between each other. The Holy Spirit was the conduit of the communication. Daniel made it very clear that there was not some unholy mind exchange or control between Daniel and Nebuchadnezzar. Daniel said, "But there is a God in heaven who reveals secrets, and He has made known to King Nebuchadnezzar" (Dan. 2:28, selections). Daniel also said, "God has made known to the king" (Dan. 2:45, selections). Nebuchadnezzar said, "Truly your God is the God of gods, the Lord of kings, *and a revealer of secrets*, since you could reveal this secret" (Dan. 2:47).

This was communication by the Holy Spirit between two people at or near the same time. This form of communication will help people to know strategies of God when there is no outward way to communicate. Testimonies have circulated of worship in China and other places where there has been extreme persecution. They just say, "We will meet where the Spirit leads." Then as the Holy Spirit leads multiple people, they join together for worship at the same time and place.

This is communication by the Holy Spirit between two people at or near the same time. This communication will help people to know strategies of God when there is no outward way to communicate.

A passage in Job expresses that kind of supernatural encounter. Job reflects a visitation from an angelic or demonic spiritual being. He discerned its presence in the night in his spirit man. He knew the communication, even though there was silence. There were no verbal words exchanged. This is biblical evidence of that type of communication:

> Now a thing was secretly brought to me, and mine ear received a little thereof. *In thoughts from the visions of the night,* when deep sleep falleth on men, Fear came upon me, and trembling, which made all my bones to shake. Then a spirit passed before my face; the hair of my flesh stood up: It stood still, but I could not discern the form thereof: an image was before mine eyes, *there was silence, and I heard a voice, saying,* shall mortal man be more just than God? Shall a man be more pure than his maker? (Job 4:12-17, KJV)

This form of communication comes in different ways and for different purposes. Jesus knew the thoughts of the Pharisees by the power of the Holy Spirit. The book of Matthew shares one such occurrence: "And at once some of the scribes *said within themselves,* 'This Man blasphemes!' *But Jesus, knowing their thoughts,* said, 'Why do you think evil in your hearts?'" (Matt. 9:3-4). There were also other times this happened in Scripture.

There are times that believers have an inner witness of the Holy Spirit with no outward form of communication. This is communication and revelation of knowledge for the purposes of God. The book of Romans says, "The Spirit Himself bears witness with our spirit that we are children of God" (Rom. 8:16), and further, "I tell the truth in Christ, I am not lying, *my conscience also bearing me witness in the Holy Spirit*" (Rom. 9:1). Believers are also led by the Spirit: "For as many as are led by the Spirit of God, these are sons of God" (Rom. 8:14). Jesus was led by the Spirit: "Then Jesus was led up by the Spirit into the wilderness to be tempted by the devil" (Matt. 4:1). Sometimes the communication may come as a check in the spirit of a person. The book of Acts says, "They were forbidden by the Holy Spirit to preach the word in Asia … They tried to go into Bithynia, but the Spirit did not permit them" (Acts 16:6-7).

Sometimes communications come in the form of visions or dreams. There were many dreams and visions in the Scripture that accelerated people into God's will. In fact, the Lord promised that in the last days dreams and visions would be a great tool for communication with the Spirit of God. The book of Joel says, "And it shall come to pass afterward that I will pour out My Spirit on all flesh; Your sons and your daughters shall prophesy, your old men shall dream dreams, your young men shall see visions; and also on My menservants and on My maidservants I will pour out My Spirit in those days" (Joel 2:28-29).

Even though we have been talking about communication that does not come audibly, there are times when believers hear the audible voice of God. Scripture is full of times that God talked to his people or even appears to them in the form of a person. God is not limited to our communication understanding. He can communicate in any manner that he deems necessary and appropriate.

One day, during a time of intense fasting and prayer, I was seeking the Lord. I was somewhat weakened by the fast, I suppose. I started to doze off. In fact, I would say that I was pretty well in a doze, but perhaps not in a sound sleep. As I sat in my chair dozing, there was a distinct tap on my arm. In fact, there were two pretty strong nudges. I was home alone so I knew that no person had touched me. I smiled at the time because I knew the Lord, probably by an angel, was communicating with me. He was saying without words, "This is too important to sleep through right now. Wake up and attend to the matter at hand!" He communicated to me without words and I had no trouble discerning his meaning. This also happened with Peter when an angel of the Lord nudged him from a sound sleep in prison: "Now behold, an angel of the Lord ... struck Peter on the side and raised him up" (Acts 12:7).

Paul taught the Corinthians about the wisdom that comes from God. He began, "However, we speak wisdom among those who are mature, yet not the wisdom of this age, nor of the rulers of this age, who are coming to nothing" (1 Cor. 2:6). Paul shared about wisdom that was not of this age. He said, "But we speak the wisdom of God in a mystery, the hidden wisdom which God ordained before the ages for our glory, which none of the rulers of this age knew; for had they known, they would not have crucified the Lord of glory" (1 Cor. 2:7-8). God has mysteries to reveal that were known before the ages began, but which are only revealed by the direction of God.

Paul quoted Isaiah 64:4 when he said, *"Eye has not seen, nor ear heard, nor have entered into the heart of man the things which God has prepared for those who love him."*

The mysteries of God were prepared before time for those who love him. That means that there are things that devoted people will receive by revelation that others will not. Those revelations come by the Spirit of God into the hearts of people. Paul said, "But God has revealed them to us through His Spirit. For the Spirit searches all things, yes, the deep things of God. For what man knows the things of a man except the spirit of the man which is in him? *Even so no one knows the things of God except the Spirit of God"* (1 Cor. 2:10-11). Because the Spirit of God is the only one who knows the things of God, the Spirit will teach his people:

> Now we have received, not the spirit of the world, but the Spirit who is from God, that we might know the things that have been freely given to us by God. These things we also speak, not in words which man's wisdom teaches but which the Holy Spirit teaches, comparing spiritual things with spiritual. But the natural man does not receive the things of the Spirit of God, for they are foolishness to him; nor can he know them, because they are spiritually discerned. But he who is spiritual judges all things, yet he himself is rightly judged by no one. For 'Who has known the mind of the Lord that he may instruct him?' But we have the mind of Christ. (1 Cor. 2:12-16)

Communication strategy will be vitally important in the days ahead. Foster spiritual hearing in ways that do not necessitate sound. The spiritual hearing is not in the ears; it is in the mind. As previously stated, however, this is talking about holy communications aided by the Holy Spirit of God. As the Lord leads, he will communicate those things that believers need to hear, when they choose to listen and respond.

Chapter 8

Overcoming the Deaf and Dumb Spirit

This is a book about revelation and how believers get strategy from hearing and receiving revelation from God. However, if people cannot hear in the spiritual realm, they will not hear the revelations of God. One of the most important verses for Israel was Deuteronomy 6:4, The Shema. It is named *shema* for the first Hebrew word in the passage, which is *Hear*! It says, "Hear, O Israel: The Lord our God, the Lord *is* one!" Hearing is critical for following the Lord! If people are spiritually deaf, they are well on their way to defeat by the enemy. Overcoming the deaf and dumb spirit is now and will later be critical for believers to walk in kingdom understanding. If people in general, and even the Church in particular, cannot hear God, they will not receive revelation for advancing God's kingdom on the earth and for end time victories over the enemy.

Make no mistake about this point: The deaf and dumb spirit is active and working in people who do not have any trouble physically speaking or hearing. This is critical for the body of believers to understand now, especially in light of knowledge and understanding that the Lord wants to give in the days ahead. If the enemy can render people spiritually deaf and mute, he can shut down the lines of communication and how people receive revelation from God.

This is already happening. It is a huge problem among believers. The deaf and dumb spirit is pervasive in the Church in the hearts and lives of believers. Most people and leaders do not recognize the impact of this spirit. If a person is operating under spiritual deafness, he or she does not know it because of the very nature of that spirit and how it operates. One in deception does not know he or she is deceived.

The main target of the deaf and dumb spirit is the spiritual functioning of the mind and release of thoughts by the vocalizations of the mouth. This spirit can and does manifest in physical muteness and deafness. However, the most pervasive manifestations of this spirit are in people who have the ability to speak and to hear in the natural realm. When the phrase *deaf and dumb* is mentioned, it is mostly presumed to be people who are physically mute or deaf. However, the main focus of this spirit is to keep people in lack of understanding. If Satan and his demons can keep people from understanding by spiritual deafness, they cannot get free and they cannot hear the truth. They cannot hear the true revelations of God.

As believers and leaders try to talk and witness to people who are in bondage to this spirit, the words are not received. It may seem as if these people are being obstinate, but they do not understand what is being said although they may hear with their ears. Jesus described this very thing when he said in the book of Mark:

> "*He who has ears to hear, let him hear!*" But when He was alone, those around Him with the twelve asked Him about the parable. And He said to them, "To you it has been given to know the *mystery of the kingdom of God*; but to those who are outside, all things come in parables, so that 'Seeing they may see and not perceive, and *hearing they may hear and not understand; lest they should turn, and their sins be forgiven them.*'" (Mark 4:9-12)

Vision of How it Works

The mind and the throat are the main targets of the deaf and dumb spirit. When the mind is bound, the person does not know that he or she is being misinformed. The Lord revealed this in a vision one morning about 4 a.m. The Lord merely said the words, "Deaf and dumb spirit." I was preparing to go to prayer anyway, so I prayed in the Spirit for about twenty or twenty-five minutes to gain understanding of what the Lord wanted to show me about the deaf and dumb spirit. Then the Lord gave me a vision in three parts.

First, I saw a metallic collar on a person's throat. The collar was bigger than a dog collar but not quite as thick as a whiplash collar. It was gray metallic and the person was bound snuggly around the neck, but not to the point of death. The inside of the collar had ivory spikes which were pointing into the person's skin. They were not breaking the skin, but they had the potential to bring pressure by pressing into the throat. At that point I did not know what I was seeing.

The first part of the vision was the binding on the neck. The throat contains the voice box, or larynx; the pharynx; the esophagus, for intake of nourishment from the mouth to the stomach through the throat; the trachea, which is for intake of air; and the jugular vein and arteries, which take blood to and from the brain. If this spirit binds the throat, and not the mouth, then it has the ability to impact a lot more than simple speech, spiritually speaking. People bound by this spirit still usually have the ability to speak with their mouths, but the spirit can limit or hinder the things that the person says or that the Lord wants to bring forth. However, the things that the enemy wants to allow can come forth without hindrance: for example, cursing, anything that goes against the will of God, or physical or vocal attacks on the people around the person who is under control of this spirit, to name a few. Spiritually speaking, when the throat is limited in functioning leading to muteness, the spiritual deafness is often not recognized.

Second, I saw the back of the neck and head. Starting at the back of the neck, I saw this collar was attached to a "skull cap." The collar/cap was connected as one apparatus which came up the back of the head, leaving the ears exposed, and covering the cranium. The apparatus was binding the throat and mind. The physical mouth and ears were exposed. When the mind is impaired, the ability to discern good from evil, the ability to understand, and the ability to receive knowledge of God are impaired. What happens if a believer is talking to a person who has no ability to discern right from wrong, good from evil, holy from unholy? What happens if someone has no ability to understand? What happens when a person is in deception?

If a person *has been* in deception, that person can look back and say, "I was deceived." However, if a person is actively in deception, that person does not know he or she is being deceived because it is deception. By the very definition of *deception*, if a person is actively being deceived at that moment, he or she cannot know it. Deceit is the act of concealing or misrepresenting the truth. People who are deceived do not know that they are being deceived. One reason why this spirit is so devastating and hard to overcome is because people do not know that they are being bound. Unfortunately, words alone are often not an effective arsenal to convince people that they have been deafened to the Word of God.

Third, I saw that the lock which required a key was on the very back part of the neck. I had the revelation that it was almost impossible for a person who was bound by the deaf and dumb spirit to get to the lock by him or herself. The Lord said that the key to open the lock was the blood of Jesus.

In the final part of the vision, the lock was on the back of the neck. The difficulty of inserting a key straight into a lock behind one's head would be very challenging. That does not even take into consideration that a person may not recognize deception enough to realize that he or she needed to use the key. If people had to free themselves, it would be very difficult and very challenging. Those people lack the understanding that they need to be delivered from that spirit. First, they lack the ability to understand the need for deliverance; and second, they lack the ability to set themselves free. The anointing of Jesus is what breaks that yoke of bondage.

There are some things that people can easily recognize the need to be free from: addiction, carnality, lust, gluttony, illness, anger, etc. People can recognize these afflictions. If they want to be free, they can engage themselves in steps to get free. People can get in the Word of God, get prayer ministry, fast, worship the Lord, yield to the Lord, seek the guidance of the Holy Spirit, walk in purity, or seek godly counsel. However, a person who is in active deception is in a different situation. It is a very challenging situation because people who are oppressed by the deaf and mute spirit need help to get free but do not recognize that fact. There are many Scriptures about hearing and understanding. There is a difference between hearing and hearing with understanding. The book of Acts says:

> Hearing you will hear, and shall not understand; and seeing you will see, and not perceive; for the hearts of this people have grown dull. Their ears are hard of hearing, and their eyes they have closed, lest they should see with their eyes and hear with their ears, lest they should understand with their hearts and turn, so that I should heal them. (Acts 28:26-27)

This verse shows that people can hear with the ears, but still lack understanding. Have you ever heard something but did not get full revelation of what was being said? I have even looked right at a person and acknowledged understanding, only to realize later that I did not *hear* them. Jeremiah 6:10 says, "To whom shall I speak and give warning, that they may hear? Indeed, their ear is uncircumcised, and they cannot give heed. Behold, the word of the Lord is a reproach to them; They have no delight in it." Further Ezekiel 12:2 says, "Son of man, you dwell in the midst of a rebellious house, which has eyes to see but does not see, and ears to hear but does not hear; for they are a rebellious house." Without understanding, there is no healing and there is no deliverance. With understanding, complete healing follows.

Leviticus 19:14 says, "You shall not curse the deaf, nor put a stumbling block before the blind, but *shall fear your God:* I am the Lord." It is very hard dealing with a person who is spiritually deaf. Although challenging, the Lord says do not curse the deaf or put a stumbling block before the blind. What is really needed is compassion. For those people who cannot spiritually hear, there must be compassion because to help them is to show fear of the Lord.

The problem with this spirit is the person who is bound by it may not be able to share enough to reveal that he or she is even bound. Furthermore, the person's mind is bound and cannot be engaged to help facilitate or participate in one's own healing or deliverance. The person has limited ability to receive wise counsel because the spiritual hearing is in the mind, which is bound. The vast majority of people who receive wisdom, revelation, and discernment from God get it first in the mind. Very rarely do people receive revelation in the ears as the audible voice of God. The deaf and dumb spirit binds the thinking. That is why in the vision the Lord gave, the mind was bound, but the ears were exposed.

When people get delivered, their thinking is clear and they are free to speak. This explains why some have been unable to receive wise counsel. Those bound cannot hear it from parents, friends, or even from the Lord. Often there is no response to conversation, or a delayed response. Spiritual muteness, which is differentiated from actual muteness, prevents the person from talking about spiritual things. Sometimes it may seem like the person wants to talk, but is not free to do so. There are times that the deaf and dumb spirit works with an orphan spirit or a spirit of error, or other spirits.

In multiple deliverance ministry sessions, I have seen people who actually wanted to speak, but could not utter the words that they wanted to say. They could talk just fine until it came to saying the name of Jesus or talking about the blood of Jesus. When I am ministering to people in that situation and I ask them to repeat something, I do not move on until they repeat exactly what I want them to say. It is not unusual to repeat a phrase several times before it is repeated properly without hindrance. The demonic opposition will make it very difficult for people to speak important words in deliverance ministry. They can talk about the weather without a problem, but when it comes to breaking ties with the enemy or talking about Jesus or his blood, it gets challenging. When that happens, I do not move on, but bind the deaf and dumb spirit from hindering their speech.

By Nothing but Prayer and Fasting

My husband preached on fasting one Sunday morning. As I prepared to go to worship with him, he told me all of the Scriptures that he was going to use in his sermon. He practically told me his entire sermon. I do not think that he even mentioned it, but I heard the Holy Spirit repeat several times in my mind, *"This kind can come out by nothing but prayer and fasting"* (Mark 9:29). I looked it up and was amazed to refresh my memory that the passage was dealing with none other than the deaf and dumb spirit. Mark 9 told the story of the young son who was burdened with the deaf and mute spirit:

> And when He came to the disciples, He saw a great multitude around them, and scribes disputing with them. Immediately, when they saw Him, all the people were greatly amazed, and running to Him, greeted Him. And He asked the scribes, "What are you discussing with them?" Then one of the crowd answered and said, "Teacher, I brought You my son, who has *a mute spirit*. And wherever it seizes him, it throws him down; he foams at the mouth, gnashes his teeth, and becomes rigid. So I spoke to Your disciples, that *they should cast it out, but they could not."*

> He answered him and said, "O faithless generation, how long shall I be with you? How long shall I bear with you? Bring him to Me." Then they brought him to Him. And when he saw Him, immediately the spirit convulsed him, and he fell on the ground and wallowed, foaming at the mouth. So He asked his father, "How long has this been happening to him?" And he said, "From childhood. And often he has thrown him both into the fire and into the water to destroy him. But if You can do anything, have." Jesus said to him, *"If you can believe, all things*

are possible to him who believes." Immediately
the father of the child cried out and said with tears,
"Lord, I believe; help my unbelief!"

When Jesus saw that the people came running
together, He rebuked the unclean spirit, saying to
it, *"Deaf and dumb spirit, I command you, come
out of him and enter him no more!"* Then the spirit
cried out, convulsed him greatly, and came out of
him. And he became as one dead, so that many said,
"He is dead." But Jesus took him by the hand and
lifted him up, and he arose.

And when He had come into the house, His disciples asked Him privately, "Why could we not *cast it
out?"* So He said to them, *"This kind can come out
by nothing but prayer and fasting."* (Mark 9:14-29)

Jesus had just come off the Mount of Transfiguration, where
he had been in the glory of God. Down below, the disciples could
not cast the deaf and mute spirit out of the boy. Jesus was under
the anointing from his encounter where he had been in the presence of the Father. There was even something about his appearance
that made him amazing to the people, "Immediately, *when they
saw Him, all the people were greatly amazed,* and running to Him,
greeted Him" (Mark 9:15). This reminds me of the time that Moses
came off the mountain from being in the presence of God. His face
shone with the glory of God so that he had to wear a veil (Exod.
34:35). Jesus was anointed for dealing with this unclean spirit. The
disciples did not have anointing at that moment.

Cast Out or Escape

There is something critical happening within this passage that
is often overlooked. The father of the boy asked Jesus why the disciples could not *"cast it out"* (Mark 9:18). Later the disciples asked
why they could not *"cast it out"* (Mark 9:28). However, Jesus

answered, "This kind *can come out by nothing but prayer and fasting*" (Mark 9:29). The Greek words are different here. The word for cast out is *ekballō* meaning to, "eject, cast out, drive out, expel, thrust out, put out, or send away." This is what the boy's father and the disciples were seeking. However, the word Jesus used is *exerchomai* and it means "to issue, come forth or come out, depart, escape, get out, or go forth."

The deaf and dumb spirit will come out on its own accord by nothing but prayer and fasting. With prayer and fasting, the host becomes so inhospitable that the thing wants to leave.

The disciples wanted to forcefully expel the thing, but they could not. Many people interpret this passage and their failure to do so by saying that the disciples had not been in prayer and fasting. That may be true, but there is more going on here than that fact alone. Jesus said something completely different. He said it *comes out*, but they wanted to *throw it out*. Jesus did not say that this kind is *cast out* by nothing but prayer and fasting. The inference seems to suggest that Jesus meant that this kind *escapes* by nothing but prayer and fasting. In other words, this kind voluntarily leaves by nothing but intentional intercession with fasting. This is a huge revelation: The deaf and dumb spirit will *come out on its own accord by nothing but prayer and fasting*. With prayer and fasting, the host becomes so inhospitable that the thing wants to leave. It *wants* to depart. It seems that a person who is laboring under the deaf and dumb spirit does not have the wherewithal to get to Jesus so that he or she can be set free. This is pervasive in the body of Christ, but others can stand in the gap until he or she can regain spiritual hearing.

Let me be clear here. There are times that a person can labor for another person to be free from spiritual bondage. I have heard some deliverance pastors say that if a person cannot participate in his or her own deliverance, then he or she cannot be delivered. That simply does not line up with Scripture. There are many biblical instances in which one person interceded for another resulting in healing or deliverance. The person who was healed or delivered did not participate on his or her own behalf. For example, the Syrophoenician woman, who had "great faith," petitioned for her demon possessed daughter (Matt. 15:21-28). The Centurion, also a man of great faith, petitioned for his servant who was ill unto death (Matt. 8:5-13). The nobleman came to Jesus for his son who had a fever and was about to die (John 4:46-54). None of those who were afflicted by demonization or illnesses in these passages participated in coming to Jesus for their own healing or deliverance. Yet even so, each one was healed and delivered when another person petitioned to Jesus for them.

There are some things to note here, however. At least in these instances, the ones who petitioned were either parents or were in authority over the ones who were in need of healing. The enemy is very legalistic and it seemed to be very important that the intercessors in the above instances had authority over the ones in bondage. The petitioners seemed to have great faith and determination. It is not true that all people who are in bondage must absolutely participate in deliverance ministry to be healed. However, if those who are bound are not in the battle, it seems to be more intense. The battle seems to require unsurpassed faith of the intercessors that will not yield to the devil!

Also there were people that Jesus raised from the dead, like the synagogue ruler's daughter (Mark 5:21-43) or the son of the widow of Nain (Luke 7:11-17). It goes without saying that dead people cannot participate in their own raising. Yet there were several people in Scripture raised from the dead by the compassion of Jesus.

The Scripture regarding the deaf and dumb spirit and of interceding with prayer and fasting for another person stands on the same biblical principles. It illustrates that people can be delivered when others pray and fast for them. This information is important for the Church to grasp, especially so that the body of Christ can get prepared to be the bride for whom Jesus is looking. Overcoming the deaf and dumb spirit is critical for the Church coming toward the end of the age.

Fasting

When there is prayer and fasting and there is enough pressure brought to bear, the demon will want to flee. Demons are weakened in prayer and fasting. When a person grows weak in the flesh from fasting, the demons also grow weak. The more a fast (with prayer) costs the person, the more it costs the enemy. In other words, if a person fasts from sodas, is that fast really hurting the enemy? Probably not. If a person fasts for 40 days from everything but water, growing very weak, how much is that fast costing the enemy?

I have heard testimonies from a man who did deliverance and healing ministry. He said that he was going to work with a seminary student who had a spirit of anger. He asked the young man to fast for ten days and then they were going to meet for prayer and deliverance ministry. He said that after fasting the demons were almost begging to go. That lines up with the Scripture about the deaf and dumb spirit. As people labor under the deaf and dumb spirit, they are unable to hear the truth. However, as other people fast and pray for the ones bound by this spirit, the spirit which hinders the spiritual hearing is weakened so that it may want to leave and the hearing may be restored.

Fasting is very important in Scripture. This book does not lend itself to a full teaching on fasting, but suffice it to say that both the Old and New Testaments are filled with plans and blessings of fasting. It increases the anointing. John Wesley and many other early generals of the faith practiced and promoted fasting. Many great generals of the faith in the common era engage or did engage in serious fasting at the beginning of or throughout their ministries.

Fasting is depravation of food, not TV or games, etc. When the flesh is impacted it gets close to a person in a way that nothing else will do. Occasionally married couples may fast from sexual relations for a period of time to engage in fasting and prayer: "Do not deprive one another except with consent for a time, that you may give yourselves to fasting and prayer; and come together again so that Satan does not tempt you because of your lack of self-control" (1 Cor. 7:5). Most usually, however, fasting is the abstinence from food and/or water for a prescribed period of time. Fasting brings power. There were three forty-day supernatural fasts in Scripture. Moses fasted for the unsurpassed revelation of God; Elijah fasted to overcome the enemy; and Jesus fasted for the power of the Holy Spirit. We fast for all three.

The Book of Isaiah says, "And it shall come to pass in that day, that his burden shall be taken away from off thy shoulder, and his yoke from off thy neck, and *the yoke shall be destroyed because of the anointing*" (Isa. 10:27, KJV). The yoke, the sign of bondage or servitude, is shattered from the anointing that comes from being in the presence of God. Fasting releases the anointing that allows the yoke of bondage to be destroyed.

The anointing comes only when a person gets beyond the limitations of the flesh. The carnal man wants to pet the flesh and allow sin to continue. Fasting crushes the flesh and opens the mind. The body will whimper and fuss at the idea of fasting because it costs something not to eat. It costs comfort. It takes someone with understanding to be able to help someone without understanding. The book of Matthew says it this way, "If the blind leads the blind, both will fall into a ditch" (Matt. 15:14b). It is worth the personal cost of the fast to crush the bondage for another person. When a person cannot participate in his or her own deliverance, as with the deaf and dumb spirit, he or she needs help from one who is not deaf and mute. There may be little or no self-will to be delivered when a person is spiritually deaf. This spirit is one of the first things that must go, then the person can participate in getting delivered from other things that may also be a hindrance to his or her spiritual walk and the ability to receive knowledge and strategy from the Lord. [15]

---

[15] https://youtu.be/k-vWMZFT1HI Video teaching by Dr. Laura Henry Harris: Overcoming the Deaf and Dumb Spirit. The teaching on the video is in greater detail than space allows for in this book.

Section Two

Principles of War

For though we walk in the flesh,
we do not war according to the flesh.
For the weapons of our warfare are not carnal
but mighty in God for pulling down strongholds.

2 Corinthians 10:3-4

Introduction[16]

G od is a God of war. Accordingly, God's people must be a people of war! The book of Exodus says, "The LORD is a man of war; The LORD is His name" (Exod. 15:3). Believers are in a spiritual campaign of epic proportions. The body of Christ is not *going to be* in a war; it is there already. Even as early as Genesis when the serpent was cursed by God, the result was hostility between the

---

[16] Some of the materials in this introduction and several chapters that follow about natural and spiritual warfare were inspired by the teachings of Joseph Carroll. He was a student of military strategy of World War II. I have no way to adequately cite his work because I received a set of compact discs of his messages from a friend. The compact discs, seemingly made from old tape recordings, did not contain any source information. The messages were probably forty years old, with one reference to "the recent *Jaws* movie," which was released in 1975. Joseph Carroll died at 83 years of age in 2008.

The friend who gave me the messages was personally acquainted with Joseph Carroll. Carroll freely disseminated his teaching materials during his lifetime and freely gave permission to copy and share his teachings. The friend who gave me the discs said that Carroll would have wanted the information shared, but would not have wanted any credit. However, professional authorship dictates that he receives credit for the things that he inspired and that I have used in this work.

His ministry is called Evangelical Institute School of Biblical Training, founded in 1972. The school is still active and may be found on the web at http://www.eibibleschool.org. He wrote a book that is his legacy: *How to Worship Jesus Christ: Experiencing His Manifest Presence,* which may be purchased at https://www.christianbook.com/worship-je-sus-christ-experiencing-manifest-presence/joseph-carroll/9780802409904/pd/409904

woman and her seed and the serpent and his seed. Genesis 3:14 says, "And I will put enmity between you and the woman, and between your seed and her Seed; He shall bruise your head, and you shall bruise His heel." The seed of the woman appears to be Jesus and all those who are his who are progressing into the fullness of God's plan, purpose, and desire. The serpent and serpent's seed appear to be Satan, his demonic forces, and the people of the earth who are under his dominion and influence, who do his work on the planet.

Further, the book of James also shows the battle lines that are drawn between the enemy and the Lord's people. James 4: 7-8 says, "Therefore submit to God. Resist the devil and he will flee from you. Draw near to God and He will draw near to you. Cleanse your hands, you sinners; and purify your hearts, you double-minded." This is evidence of the conflict between God's people and Satan himself. The end result is that believers are called to be humble, in submission to God, to draw near to him, and to cleanse and purify themselves. The Lord defeated the enemy, but the foes of God are still fugitives-at-large for believers to overcome.

After engaging in serious warfare with the enemy, we often find ourselves in a better place than we were before the battle. We learned to walk in triumph; we are trained for war; we are strengthened, pruned, and purified; we learned perseverance; and we find ourselves more spiritually and morally developed than before the spiritual battle. The brilliance and superiority of Christ's triumph are often revealed in our battles.

Satan is not as big as some people make him out to be, but people must not underestimate our enemy either. Believers are in a fight with the devil. Our enemy knows how to be strategic much more than we do. Believers have been pummeled by the enemy because the enemy and his forces have been much more organized than God's people, but that is going to change! The enemy forces have been at this battle for thousands of years before current believers were even born. The enemy forces are like Goliath: battle hardened and experienced as warriors, who have strategic and tactical maneuvers well in hand. But believers, like the young David, come to the battle undeveloped in the arts of war and with minimal experience, but with a true and powerful stone in our hand. Believers can appropriate the words of David in the battle against our enemy:

> You come to me with a sword, with a spear, and with a javelin. *But I come to you in the name of the Lord of hosts,* the God of the armies of Israel, whom you have defied. *This day the Lord will deliver you into my hand,* and I will strike you and take your head from you. And this day I will give the carcasses of the camp of the Philistines to the birds of the air and the wild beasts of the earth, that all the earth may know that there is a God in Israel. Then all this assembly shall know that the Lord does not save with sword and spear; *for the battle is the Lord's, and He will give you into our hands.* (1 Sam. 17:45-47)

Believers fight a real enemy, but the battle belongs to the Lord. The body of Christ fights successfully only when fighting with the plans and strategies of God that must be employed. There is a strategy of God in all of this. God will use the battles to perfect his vessels and form believers into the instruments that he wants them to be. Believers must fight it out and the victory of Christ will be made known through the body of Christ as his instruments. Believers must fight it out and the victory of Christ will be made known through the body of Christ as his instruments. First Peter says,

> Be sober, be vigilant; because your adversary the devil walks about like a roaring lion, seeking whom he may devour. *Resist him, steadfast in the faith, knowing that the same sufferings are experienced by your brotherhood in the world.* But may the God of all grace, who called us to His eternal glory by Christ Jesus, *after you have suffered a while, perfect, establish, strengthen, and settle you.* To Him

be the glory and the dominion forever and ever.
Amen. (1 Pet. 5:8-11)

The end result of the conflict is for believers to be perfect, established, strengthened, and settled. God's desire is to see believers
mature in the faith and often these battles result in spiritual growth.
The army of God is in warfare with Satan, but there is a kingdom
use for it. Ephesians 6 tells believers to put on the whole armor of
God to be able to stand against the wiles of the devil. This is war
and there are open hostilities with the enemy. Believers need to be
offensive and not merely defensive. It honors God when his army
is ready for warfare. Also as is seen in Ephesians, believers battle
only by being *"strong in the Lord and in the power of His might"*
(Eph. 6:10).

For believers to be useful to the Lord, their willingness, strength,
weaknesses, and understanding are required. We must rely on the
Lord, but there are some things that we can learn and do that will
make us more effective in the battle. Believers, led by generals,
are going to have to learn strategy much more than our ancestors
in the faith and even seek to strategically outwit and outmaneuver
our enemy. God has taught us throughout Scripture how to be strategic in warfare. There are some basic principles of war that God's
army on the earth can learn that will make us more effective in the
battles with the enemy's army.

In military warfare, the principles of war are critical for all
soldiers to know. They are also critical for the soldiers in the army
of God to know. They are objective, offensive, cooperation, networking, intelligence, line of supply, pursuit, mobility, economy
of force, and focus. Learning these tactics will help believers to
follow godly leadership and to be more strategic about fighting
the enemy, who knows a great deal about strategy. Some of these
principles of war are well known strategies by militaries around
the world, others are my own creation by the guidance of the Holy
Spirit. Being in alignment with these principles also helps us to
listen better and to know what to do when the Lord speaks his
strategy to us.

These principles work in conjunction with the knowledge of God that he gives when believers listen to him. The generals on the pages of Scripture had both parts of the equation. First, they had divine revelation of God's plans and strategies; and second, they had well-organized and disciplined armies. They could not have implemented the strategies of God with an undisciplined band of ruffians, who did not follow orders in the heat of battle. The battles facing current and future believers will require both the strategy of God and the strong discipline of a well-led army under an apostolic leader.

Jehoshaphat sought the Lord when three armies were opposing him. The Lord gave the strategy to a prophet named Jahaziel, the son of Zechariah, when the Spirit of the Lord came upon him (2 Chron. 20:14, and following verses). Jahaziel gave the word to the king, but the orchestration of the people came at the word of the firmly established leader, King Jehoshaphat. There was a firm chain of command and no confusion erupted because of the way the prophetic word came and the way the king handled it.

In the following chapters, there will be some instruction on how to handle the body of believers in the heat of an intense situation. This teaching will lend itself to understand how to use the strategy and knowledge that the Lord will give in the most effective and orderly way for the advancement of God's kingdom. It is time to transition from understanding the knowledge of God to learning about the principles of warfare. The principles of war will make the implementation of God's knowledge more effective in the battle against the enemy, Satan. We can look at the knowledge of God as intelligence information (as in spy and espionage, if you will) and the strategies learned in this section on warfare principles as how to use the intelligence more effectively.

Chapter 9

God's Plan for Strategy

Kingdom strategy leads to the culmination of all that the Lord wants to see happen on the earth. Strategy is the way to get there. The Lord's strategies are often not human strategies because his ways are higher than our ways and his thoughts are higher than our thoughts (Isa. 55:8). The Lord obviously knows more than people know, so he can form a more excellent strategy. People try to plan and make agendas based on their own understanding. Those agendas may be flawed from the beginning because they are not based on full knowledge of the circumstances and situations. The Lord has the plan, and if people will simply seek and follow his plan, the victory is sure.

Strategy is a plan of action or policy designed to achieve a major or overall aim. Strategy is the master plan or grand design of God's program. Strategy is the art of planning and directing overall military operations and movements in a war or battle.[17] We are in a battle. This is a battle of kingdom proportions, and it will take all hands on deck to have the victory. The victory will be intense because the battle will be intense. People who are listening to the Lord know that the battles have already intensified and that we will have to be dedicated to have the victory.

---

[17] https://www.google.com/?client=safari&channel=mac_bm#channel=mac_bm&q=strategy Accessed May 20, 2017

The word *strategic* means relating to the identification of long-term or overall aims and interests and the means of achieving them.[18] To be strategic means that the goals are planned, shrewd, tactical, and sometimes may even be covert. A key component of strategy is planning. Some leaders in the body are planning for a long-term overall aim. Good strategy must not be implemented without the Spirit of the Lord, or it will fail. For the plan to be crafted with success, the plan must continuously be bathed in prayer and formed only after hearing from God.

There are also biblical examples of times when people suffered sound defeat because they would not listen and follow the Word of the Lord. The Lord gives a victory every time people do as he says, albeit to wait, to go, to seek, to pray, to battle, or even to sleep. People who cannot trust God and walk in fear, play right into the enemy's plans. When people are in faith, belief, and willing to yield, victory is sure ... sure every time! The strategy of the Lord is a mixture of his will and human effort. The parts of the plan come together to form a perfect storm to defeat the plan of the enemy.

God's Will

Kingdom strategy is in the Lord's heart. Believers must seek the heart of the Lord to seek the strategy of the Lord. A heart dedicated to seeking God's kingdom and dominion will find the will of God. A heart dedicated to find God's kingdom will continue to seek his will with all strength. Seeking the kingdom of God and righteousness will lead to the addition of everything needed to walk in victory. The book of Matthew says:

> Now if God so clothes the grass of the field, which today is, and tomorrow is thrown into the oven, will He not much more clothe you, O you of little faith? "Therefore do not worry, saying, 'What shall we eat?' or 'What shall we drink?' or 'What shall we wear?' For after all these things the Gentiles

---

[18] https://www.google.com/?client=safari&channel=mac_bm#channel=mac_bm&q=strategic Accessed May 20, 2017

seek. For your heavenly Father knows that you need all these things. *But seek first the kingdom of God and His righteousness, and all these things shall be added to you.* Therefore, do not worry about tomorrow, for tomorrow will worry about its own things. Sufficient for the day is its own trouble. (Matt. 6:30-34)

The strategy of God is in the heart of God. People who really want to get the kingdom strategy must walk into a deep relationship with the Lord. Biblical examples support the idea that the Lord does not give strategy to people who do not know him or who do not want to know him. Acts 13:22 says of the Lord, "And when He had removed (King Saul), He raised up for them David as king, *to whom also He gave testimony* and said, 'I have found David the son of Jesse, *a man after my own heart, who will do all my will.*'" The person after God's heart is the one who is obedient to do the will of God. Those who show love and devotion to the Lord are the ones who obey his will: "For this is the love of God, that we keep His commandments. And His commandments are not burdensome" (1 John 5:3).

Humanity is made in the image of God and the throne of God in the lives of humanity is in the heart. God is seeking wholehearted love and devotion from people who seek after the heart of God. There are some people who just have a heart to go after God! They are going to seek him with their whole being and they will do whatever it takes to seek him. That means that they seek God and do his will, which requires obedience. He who loves the Lord, seeks to obey him. God gives testimony, as he did with David in Acts 13:22, about people who seek and find his heart. In Acts 13, it was the Lord himself who spoke of David's desire to find and know the heart of God. David's whole-hearted devotion must have pleased God very much indeed for him to witness about David on the pages of Scripture. In fact, did God ever give witness or testimony about any other person in Scripture in that way?

When we pray the will of God we know that he hears us and that we shall have the answer that we have sought: "Now this is the confidence that we have in Him, *that if we ask anything according to His will, He hears us. And if we know that He hears us, whatever we ask, we know that we have the petitions that we have asked of Him*" (1 John 5:14-15). It is powerful, effective, and absolutely critical that we seek the will of God!

The end time strategy will be intense. I previously recounted a word the Lord gave me that several people will have knowledge of different parts of God's end time strategy. The parts of it will fit together like the pieces of a puzzle. However, if there is no unity among believers, the strategy will not be fully revealed! The Lord also said that partial or incomplete information can be worse than no information at all.

I thought of the movie *Crimson Tide* with actors Denzel Washington and Gene Hackman. The movie focused on a clash of wills between the two officers on a submarine arising from conflicting interpretations of an order to launch their nuclear missiles. The order was only partially received due to a disruption in the radio service halfway through the receipt of the message. One leader interpreted the message to launch the warheads. The other officer said the message was not clear so the missiles should not be launched. Obviously, the ramifications of the decision were worldwide. The whole movie was based on the explosion of chaos on the submarine because of the uncertainty of the order. The generals in the central command had the full knowledge of the situation and the full plan of action. However, the officers on the submarine had only the partial information they received from an incomplete message. The image of the chaos on the submarine is a good example of what can happen in the body of Christ when God's army has incomplete or partial information.

There was also confusion in the leadership. The two officers were battling for control of the vessel and therefore the right to control the launch of the warheads. Each one thought with strong, heartfelt conviction that he was right. There was no wrong motive in either of the men, only confusion in the understanding of their order. This scenario should speak to the leaders in the body of Christ, who believe with conviction that they are correct but are in disunity with others in the body of Christ. Unity in understanding is vital and the Holy Spirit will lead. Knowledge, listening and hearing, and unity are critical to keep order and be effective. Otherwise, the body of Christ will be in chaos.

Since the Lord told me that many people would have parts of the plan and strategy, I have seen that come to pass. Several times, as if the Lord was using these opportunities to teach and show me, people have had partial information but did not know what it meant. The Lord had already given me an answer to their need for more information. The issue of the African man with the dream in 2011, in an earlier chapter, is just one example. Many people have had pieces of the puzzle but could not form a full understanding of what the Lord wanted them to know. They had partial information, and I had partial information. When the two ideas came together, the plan was fully formed.

Apostolic leadership will be vitally important to bring the body of Christ into order. In the days ahead, the body of Christ will have to understand that we do not have the full picture and that there is not going to be one person who will have full understanding. Of course there will be leaders, but leaders will help people to walk out their call in the final battle of the end of the age. There must be unity in the camp. There must be reliance on the will and Word of the Lord. Believers cannot know his will if they cannot hear him. The Lord, as we see in the type of the strategic generals in the movie, knows the entire plan. He can see the whole theater of battle, but the soldiers cannot. The book of Isaiah shares this idea well:

> *"For My thoughts are not your thoughts, nor are your ways My ways,"* says the Lord. "For as the heavens are higher than the earth, so are My ways higher than your ways, and My thoughts than your thoughts. "For as the rain comes down, and the snow from heaven, and do not return there, but water the earth, and make it bring forth and bud, that it may give seed to the sower and bread to the eater, *so shall My word be that goes forth from My mouth; It shall not return to Me void, but it shall*

accomplish what I please, and it shall prosper in the thing for which I sent it. (Isa. 55:8-11)

Human Effort

Those with strategy have the big picture plan. A battle is not won in chaos or disorder. Generals can win with an inferior force when they have a superior plan. God is not so limited: He has both a superior force and a superior plan. However, if his superior force does not tap into his superior plan by listening and receiving his orders, a lesser force with a good plan may carry the day. When people are in discord and are not organized in their attack against the enemy forces, they are often defeated. Only when human effort is joined with the Lord's will and plan will the human effort be successful on a kingdom scale.

The supernatural will be the norm. Indeed, the supernatural of God must be the norm! For if it is not supernatural, then by default it is natural. Humanity can accomplish the natural victory alone without God's guidance and strength. On the other hand, the evidence of the natural must also be the standard because the natural must be combined in the strategic plan with the supernatural. It is true that God and humanity will join together in unity to overcome the-defeated-but-still-fighting enemy.

Throughout history, the Lord has used many great individuals who sacrificed much to serve him and do his will. This book was written around the time of the 500th anniversary of the Protestant Reformation, which was birthed by the actions of reformer Martin Luther. Believers can look back and celebrate those who have gone before and what they have brought into reality as God's plan joined with their human effort. It was hard on Martin Luther. He swam against the tide of big religion when he took on a war with the Catholic Church. He nailed ninety-five theses on the door of the church at Wittenberg, Germany in 1517. Those strikes of the hammer released the sounds of change that have never been recalled. By his actions, he released the great transformation of faith that was a watershed moment in Church history. His efforts against the established religious culture were very hard. He was a forerunner of change. Forerunners often go against the tide and they are often not understood. He suffered for his call.

The Lord spoke to me and said, "It was a hard call but he carried it well and *it wrought great change*." Wrought was an interesting word that is not found in my normal vocabulary. I looked it up in the dictionary. I learned this about the word:

> Wrought metals are those that have been shaped by hammers and other tools, as opposed to cast metals, which are melted into a mold, or extruded metals, which are forced through a die. This is one of the oldest metalworking techniques; the word "wrought" actually comes from a form of "to work," so wrought metal is "worked" metal.[19]

Before looking it up, I did not know that wrought had to do with beating the metal. Luther wrought change. It was intensely hot and not without pain. In essence, it was taking a situation, and by the application of heat and pressure, forced it into a different shape. Think of the Protestant Reformation in those terms for a while.

The Hammer and Anvil of Kingdom Warfare

This talk of wrought metal also made me think of the hammer and anvil. Those are instruments to hammer hot metal into the shape that the blacksmith desires. The anvil is the heavy, hard steel or iron block which the hot metal is laid against to apply the hammer. The hammer is the instrument of pressure.

When I looked up the hammer and anvil, I also learned another interesting point. The *Hammer and Anvil* is a simple, yet effective and strategic, tactic in military war. It begins with two opposing infantry forces engaging in a frontal assault. While the infantry lines are fixed in the engagement, the home-team cavalry maneuvers around the enemy to attack from behind, sandwiching the

---

[19] https://www.google.com/?client=safari&channel=mac_bm#channel=mac_bm&q=wrought Accessed May 20, 2017

enemy into the friendly infantry.[20] The cavalry charges and then pulls back to reorganize. The cavalry continues the process of assault and pull back to regroup until the enemy is pulverized by the relentless assaults. The front-line infantry is the anvil or the hard immovable object and the cavalry is the hammer.

In many ways the body of Christ is learning military strategy. We must learn it well as it will help us not only to survive but also to be victorious to the end. Our enemy is very strategic, but our side has often not learned to be strategic. Military strategy only works when the troops are disciplined and in formation. Leadership is key. Unity is a key component to any military strategy. To teach strategy to many, leaders have to understand the meaning of it first. Strategy of knowledge is a great theory, but unless there is unity in the application of the concept, it will be "every man for himself."

Strategy will not be effective until all troops are working in unity and every person is in his or her proper place. Military strategy will be the second part of this book and it will help apostolic leaders know how to organize the troops. We have learned that a big part of the strategy is listening to the Lord, our central command, and following his orders. We will know more as we learn to listen well. When we hear and follow his lead, we will know his plan. That level of hearing will be critical in the days ahead - for everyone.

Hammer and anvil: I think of "Heat it and beat it." Heat has to be applied to the metal for the hammer and anvil to be effective.

In essence it is catching the heated metal between a hard spot and a hammer. That works on the enemy too! We must ask: Lord, how do we catch the enemy between a hard spot and the hammer? What is the anvil in strategic spiritual warfare and what is the hammer?

The anvil is the Lord. He is the hard spot; the unbending and resolute object which will not be moved. The body of well-organized believers under firm apostolic leadership is the hammer, the forces of the earth in God's army.

Think of the placement of the enemy in the second heavenly

---

[20] https://en.wikipedia.org/wiki/Hammer_and_anvil

realm. The anvil is the Lord. He is the hard spot; the unbending and resolute object which will not be moved. The body of well-organized believers under firm apostolic leadership is the hammer, the forces of the earth in God's army. The Lord applies the heat and believers apply the pressure. The heat is released by the prayers of the people. The kitchen gets very hot for the enemy when people start praying. The battering ram of the earth in prayer, fasting, worship, praise, devotion, obedience to God pummels the enemy between the hammer and the hard spot. God is never changing. Humanity is the only variable. When believers are praying in unity and applying the hammer, so to speak, the enemy is caught in a very difficult and defeated position. The enemy is then hemmed in on every side and ineffective in their attempts at warfare on the earth. This will only work in unity and the body being of one accord.

God is giving the body of believer's strategy in the hammer and anvil tactic. Has it ever been very effectively used in spiritual warfare? Have we ever seen warfare exactly in this way? People have not known about it. The camps of warfare strategy and kingdom strategy have not come together, but we must do so now!

There is a biblical example of the Hammer and Anvil as seen in Joshua 8. Joshua set ambushes and drew the men of Ai out and then attacked them from behind. Joshua ambushed Ai by making them think Israel was retreating so that they would come out and pursue them, which is exactly what happened. When the people of Ai left the city unattended, the rear guard captured the city and burned it. Then all the troops of Israel surrounded the army of Ai and decimated them. This is a classic case of sandwiching the enemy between two contingent forces of the home team. The warriors of Ai were caught by surprise and hemmed in before and behind. They were soundly defeated by a better strategy and a superior fighting force and none escaped. Believers can do this to the enemy when we are dedicated to being in unity and committed to the cause of spiritual and military strategy based on the knowledge of God.

Chapter 10

Objective

An objective is the target, goal, or sought after conclusion. In any warfare situation, it is necessary to have a clearly defined objective. Otherwise, the troops may wander aimlessly never coming to an appointed end or victory. How will believers ever gauge success if they have no goal in mind in their endeavors to serve God? The objectives may be either immediate objectives or the ultimate or end objective. It is important to have a clearly defined purpose in mind, so that every effort is working toward that goal.

I spent twenty years as an attorney in a small town legal practice. I spent a great amount of time in the courtroom representing clients to prove and win their cases. In a court of law, there are certain facts that have to be proven to win a case. A savvy attorney will not ask questions or present evidence except that it points only to the facts that must be proven to win the case. The same is true in establishing strategy toward meeting an immediate, intermediate, or ultimate objective. If there is an objective, any action that does not point to the fulfillment of that objective is a wasted effort.

Any objective that is established must be clear and concise, so there is no possibility of a mistake. Objectives should be articulated with few words. In fact, the fewer, the better. Simple language is best. The clearly defined objective is established by the commander. In the army of the Lord, as in any military situation, soldiers live to obey the commander. The ultimate commander is Jesus Christ! However, the ordained commander in the New Testament church is the apostle, who only has that title by right if called by Christ, and not self-proclaimed.

The commander or apostolic leader sets the objective that the soldiers are to carry out. Apostles clearly establish doctrine in Scripture (Acts 2:42). Apostles are not called to be dictatorial or tyrannical autocrats, but there were firm leaders established by God in the Bible. The apostles lead and give understanding of the orders to fulfill the objectives. Soldiers in the army obey the Lord, or his truly ordained leaders, without question. That sounds harsh, but it happened that way on the pages of Scripture from beginning to end. Believers who love the Lord will also obey when the authentic God-given leader releases an assignment from God. In an intense battle, lives are saved and objectives are met by people responding without question when an order is given. In the army of God in this age, the apostles are the commanders who will set the objectives of the body of Christ. The problem comes when everyone wants to be a leader, and cannot or will not yield to the God-appointed leader. There was one Moses; there was one Joshua; and there was one Paul. Each of those leaders had leaders under them, but in those instances there was one primary leader appointed by God to be the top-dog leader. They did not lead by committee or vote.

Even so, leaders are under the leadership of other apostolic leaders. This is not about a hierarchy, but rather about a system of accountability. In fact, apostolic leaders are called to be the greatest servants of all. Jesus demonstrated servant-leadership, and his appointed leaders of this age are no different. There was strong discipline in Scripture for those who disobeyed the leader. Achan in Joshua 7 brought sin into the camp by bringing in articles of false worship which were devoted to other gods. He disobeyed a direct order of God, as stated by his general, Joshua. He paid for that disobedience with his life and the lives of his family. Obedience matters: It saves lives and it honors God.

This is not about a hierarchy, but rather about a system of accountability. In fact, apostolic leaders are called to be the greatest servants of all.

Obedience is how believers show love and devotion to the Lord: "Behold, to obey is better than sacrifice, and to heed than the fat of rams" (1 Sam. 15:22). Further, 1 John says, "For this is the love of God, that we keep His commandments. And His commandments are not burdensome" (1 John 5:3). The objective of God is fulfilled when we have finished the work that the Lord has given us to do. When the defined purpose that the Lord has given us is fulfilled, our destiny ordained by God is fulfilled.

Jesus had some stated and clearly defined objectives on the earth. First, he was to destroy the works of the devil: "He who sins is of the devil, for the devil has sinned from the beginning. For this *purpose, the Son of God was manifested, that He might destroy the works of the devil*" (1 John 3:8). Second, Jesus was sent to preach the kingdom of God: "But (Jesus) said to them, 'I must preach the kingdom of God to the other cities also, because *for this purpose I have been sent*'" (Luke 4:43). Third, Jesus was sent to be the atoning sacrifice to the Father for the people: "Now My soul is troubled, and what shall I say? 'Father, save Me from this hour?' *But for this purpose I came to this hour*" (John 12:27), and further revealed in Acts, "Him, being delivered by *the determined purpose and foreknowledge of God*, you have taken by lawless hands, have crucified, and put to death" (Acts 2:23).

The Holy Spirit also has some stated objectives on the earth. He brings conviction to the world: "And when (the Holy Spirit) has come, He will convict the world of sin, and of righteousness, and of judgment: of sin, because they do not believe in Me; of righteousness, because I go to My Father and you see Me no more; of judgment, because the ruler of this world is judged" (John 16:8-11). He transforms believers in the sight of God: "And such were some of you. But you were washed, but you were sanctified, but you were justified in the name of the Lord Jesus and by the Spirit of our God" (1 Cor. 6:11). He helps believers to remember the words of Jesus: "But the Helper, the Holy Spirit, whom the Father will send in My name, He will teach you all things, and bring to your remembrance all things that I said to you" (John 14:26). The Spirit of God helps believers to lead a godly life: "But the fruit (evidence) of the Spirit is love, joy, peace, longsuffering, kindness, goodness, faithfulness, gentleness, self-control. Against such there is no law" (John 14:26). He gives the body of Christ spiritual gifts for the edification of believers: "There are diversities of gifts, but the same Spirit. There are differences of ministries, but the same Lord. And there are diversities of activities, but it is the same God who works all in all. But the manifestation of the Spirit is given to each one for the profit of all" (1 Cor. 12:4-7).

The Father "Is." I do not know if there is a stated purpose of the Father on earth other than he simply "Is." He is Creator; he loves us. I cannot state those as being his stated purposes or objectives, the reason for his existence. It really seems to be overreaching and unnecessary to proclaim and define that God has a stated purpose! HE IS!

Having said that, at least two parts of the Godhead have stated purposes while on the earth for their respective missions and ministries. If they have stated objectives, why should humanity, who is made in the image of God, be any different? Perhaps the best attempt to identify the ultimate objective of humanity was given by Jesus in the Great Commission:

> And Jesus came and spoke to them, saying, "All authority has been given to Me in heaven and on earth. *Go therefore and make disciples of all the nations, baptizing them in the name of the Father and of the Son and of the Holy Spirit, teaching them to observe all things that I have commanded you*; and lo, I am with you always, even to the end of the age." Amen. (Matt. 28:18-20)

Within that ultimate objective, undoubtedly the Lord will reveal immediate or intermediate objectives for individual believers. I recently heard a powerful bishop from Zambia preach a sermon stating that a *nation* should be our smallest objective because the Lord told us to make disciples of all nations in the Great Commission. It is true that when we seek a mere community, we are seeking too small because the Lord has told us to go after the world.

In the first section of the book, the message of the Lord was to teach how to listen. The goal was to learn to seek him for strategy and understanding and knowledge by listening. When believers

114

listen and hear, he will set our objectives, both immediate and long-range. Those objectives should fit within the larger framework of the body of Christ because God is the God of order. I will give the caveat, however, that there are times when God clearly gives an objective that is intent on bringing disorder, at least for a season of time. Or at least, disorder is the manifestation of the work toward reaching that objective. The objective should always fit within the larger framework of God's kingdom order. Even those who bring disorder to ungodly systems should be in the larger framework of order in God's kingdom.

Elsewhere in this book, there is a discussion of Martin Luther. He created great disruption, but the end result was for a purpose of God. The book of Acts is full of people seeking the objectives of God, yet they were disruptive to the established religious systems. Many of those believers were persecuted. Even when persecution comes, the objective of God must be kept in full vision.[21] Believers should look to the finale with the goal to be able to say to the Lord, "I have finished the work that you have given me to do." Even when the battle is the toughest, there is a wonderful feeling of having done the will of God. Paul talked about finishing the race with joy. Paul kept the stated objective in mind, but he created havoc with the ungodly establishment at the same time:

> But none of these things move me; nor do I count my life dear to myself, so that I may finish my race with joy, and the ministry which I received from the Lord Jesus, to testify to the gospel of the grace of God. "And indeed, now I know that you all, among whom I have gone preaching the kingdom of God, will see my face no more. (Acts 20:24-25)

The objective is important but it must be borne out of love and devotion to the Lord. Devotion is what the Lord seeks from his people. Part of our objective is to be devoted to God. Joseph Carroll said, "To know him is to love him; to love him is to obey

---

[21] See teaching video by Dr. Laura Henry Harris on Faith, Perseverance, and Vision. https://youtu.be/U6rDWxTlY1U

him, and to obey him is to prove that we love him."[22] It is somewhat of a circular argument, but it adequately makes the point that if we want to show love and devotion to the Lord, we will accomplish the objectives that he has given us to accomplish.

There are times that fulfilling the objective of God extracts a high price. It is personally costly. Salvation is free, but discipleship (in fulfilling the objective of God) is not. When costly decisions must be made to fulfill the objective of God, it is necessary to subjugate the flesh and personal desires. Fulfillment of God's objective is more important than any personal wish or desire that we have, even the preservation of life itself. Discipline is key to meeting the objective of God.

Satan will try to distract believers from the God-given objective. Biblical examples of this are seen in all the ways that Pharaoh tried to distract and negotiate with Moses in the book of Exodus. Moses had an assignment to take the people three day's journey into the wilderness to worship God. God had a stated objective, but the enemy leader wanted to change that assignment by saying do not take your livestock, or do not take your families, or do not go so far, etc. A clearly defined objective will be more easily fulfilled than if no objective is stated. When believers know the Lord and know his purpose, there will be more dedication to seeing it through. The Lord is here to train believers to know his kingdom plan. Satan is constantly trying to turn God's people aside from the objective of God. It does not matter how he brings the distraction; if he gets believers off the objective, he has won.

When believers learn to listen, they should expect the Lord to show a clearly defined and unmistakable objective. It is about knowing the will of God and seeking to have it fulfilled in the lives of humanity. The humility of a person will help define the objective. God draws near to the humble but resists the proud. In his nearness, his words will be more evident and clear. Live in the will of God, according to the Word of God, and he will guide those who will listen and follow his objective. When he shows a person what to do, it should be done with immediate obedience. The safest place to be is in the will of God, even if it means death to the flesh.

---

[22] See previous footnote about Joseph Carroll.

Chapter 11

Offensive

The last chapter discussed the need for a clearly defined military objective. The long-term objective is in the fulfillment of the Great Commission. Multiple short-term objectives leading to the ultimate objective depend on the calling that the Lord has given each one. How do we approach fulfilling the objective? The answer is to go on the offensive, which is believers going on the attack in a military campaign against the enemy. Offensive is the way that believers take charge of any situation. Believers have to take the offensive to deliver the world from the grip of the enemy, who has taken the earth and humanity captive. The enemy has aggressively advanced his cause on the earth and it is up to believers to wake up and to advance against his position. Offense is an attitude as well as an action. In warfare or in prayer, one should never take on a defensive or passive attitude. Those who try to hunker down and hold a position are often defeated.

Look at a basketball game, for example. How many times has a team jumped out to a decisive lead, then only to focus on the clock and try to stall the game to let the seconds tick away? Often, the team that is in the lead does not take shots when they are presented and they end up losing the ball. The other team is able to score and come back. It has happened time and again. It is a passive strategy that often leads to defeat. The winning team goes from being on the offensive to playing defensive ball. I have always heard the old adage, "Dance with the one who brung you!" That is southern backwoods slang, which means to keep doing what you did to get you in the lead to begin with. That means when a team is ahead, it should not back off, instead it should press harder.

My husband and I are trial lawyers. We learned very early in our legal careers that cases that were prepared for trial were the ones that most often settled out of court. My husband was handling a serious injury case for a very sweet older lady. The case appeared to be pretty cut and dried in terms of liability. There was another attorney who represented another injured party. That attorney went in with the attitude that his case would settle out of court, so he never prepared the case. My husband aggressively prepared his case for trial, assuming that the case would not settle. In the end, my husband's case settled out of court for a very favorable settlement, but the other case did not settle and the attorney had to take the case to trial. The difference was being aggressive versus being passive. That is what it means to be on the offensive.

There are some rules of offensive that believers must know and understand, which will be discussed in this chapter. Believers must not let the enemy stretch the battle lines. Believers must set the stage of the engagement, and not let the enemy set the battle on his terms. Believers must avoid unnecessary battles, as well as dangerous or distracting emotional involvements. Believers must know our enemy, and therefore be more effective in battle.

In military warfare there are two basic ways to be on the offensive: To take the whole battlefront simultaneously or to engage against one segment of the opposing army. An army can have overwhelming strength at one designated point in the battle or they can spread out and try to have a complete victory over the entire opposing force. To attack the whole line in a full frontal assault, one must have overwhelming superiority.

Our enemy will create a distraction that will attempt to use up all of the reserves and resources. If he cannot win the battle, he is about as effective in keeping people at war and worn out so that the body if Christ cannot attend to its own offensives, but is on the defensive all the time. When the battle line is extended and the home-team is fighting on every front, there are sure to be weaknesses somewhere along the battle line. The enemy knows our weaknesses and he is sure to attack hardest in the weak spots. The caution is to use wisdom to not extend the battle line too far. Cover what can be adequately covered. Extend the line only when breakthrough can be achieved in one area. In other words, concentrate only on the assignments given by the Lord. Fight the battles that he has called forth to fight. Protect the weak spots so that the enemy cannot hit there causing the whole defense to collapse.

Do not waste time by fighting unnecessary battles. Believers should not be tempted to take on a war with the enemy that they have not been called to fight. People end up getting hurt when they wander into battlegrounds that they have not been called to go into by the Lord. When the Lord calls one to a particular battle, there is grace for the journey. We must not be diverted into unnecessary battles that have not been called forth by central command. One strategy of the enemy is to try to get God's people fighting on so many fronts so that the defenses finally break.

There is also the idea and understanding of anointing for the call. It has often been said, "The higher the level, the bigger the devil." In other words, people are promoted and advanced by the Lord. People have certain levels of anointing for certain battles. In God's army, there are privates, or new believers and immature Christians who have never advanced or been promoted. There are also generals who have been tried and tested by the Lord and who are ready to take on high-level warfare. There is every level in between those two. Generals have anointing for higher level warfare than do the privates. I say this to say that when people go on the offensive beyond their level of anointing, it is very dangerous. They are outside of their calling and they can be unprotected. Believers are called to be aggressive and on the offensive in the level of calling and anointing given by the Lord. People who get beyond their call, often end up hurt or dead. Seriously. I have seen death result when people have taken on battles beyond their anointing and maturity.

In one example, there was a young man who took on a battle against a very serious principality. He was very eager to serve the Lord, but what he possessed in eagerness, he may have lacked in wisdom. I saw him early one morning as he was praying at a very serious demonic stronghold in our area. I circled back around to

Taking the offensive in a battle that we have not been called by the Lord to fight is very dangerous. However, when the Lord has called forth the battle, we can proceed with utmost confidence that we are doing the right thing in following his will and his call.

give him a warning that I felt was from the Lord. The warning was not to go before the Lord into this battle, but to wait until the Lord was ready to make the charge against this principality. The young man plowed ahead in a very public display to have some apparent demonic markings removed from a public building. The historical society was up in arms; the government officials were up in arms. But even more importantly, the demonic realm was up in arms.

He was a young pastor and a very good one. He was very eloquent in his delivery and gave powerful and discerning messages. Very soon after he began that frontal attack on a demonic principality, he developed cancer that attacked his throat. It was an attack on his ability to serve as pastor and seemed to be directly related to his attack on the demonic principality. The primary instrument that a pastor uses is his voice. That was his tool to use for the kingdom of God, and that was the point of attack of the enemy against his life. He battled to regain his health for two or three years. Ultimately, he died as a very young man.

A biblical example is seen in the story of the seven sons of Sceva. They took on a battle for which they were not prepared or called to fight. They were soundly defeated in the process. In Acts, the demons did not recognize their authority and arose in fury against the sons. The book of Acts says:

> Then some of the itinerant Jewish exorcists took it upon themselves to call the name of the Lord Jesus over those who had evil spirits, saying, "We exorcise you by the Jesus whom Paul preaches." Also there were seven sons of Sceva, a Jewish chief

priest, who did so. And the evil spirit answered and said, "*Jesus I know, and Paul I know; but who are you?*" Then the man in whom the evil spirit was leaped on them, overpowered them, and prevailed against them, so that they fled out of that house naked and wounded. (Acts 19:13-16)

Taking the offensive in a battle that we have not been called by the Lord to fight is very dangerous. However, having given that testimony, I will say when the Lord has called forth the battle, we can proceed with utmost confidence that we are doing the right thing in following his will and his call. If God calls us into a dangerous battle, he will go before us and he will cover us from behind. The book of Isaiah says, "For you shall not go out with haste, nor go by flight; For the *LORD will go before you, And the God of Israel will be your rear guard*" (Isa. 52:12). Believers can go into a battle that the Lord has called us to, even against overwhelming odds with confidence.

Another area of concern in going on the offensive is when a person of God stumbles into sin. There can be flesh or emotional traps that are exposed and the person falls. Having open sin is especially dangerous when there is a frontal offensive battle going on. The enemy will look for any weakness to expose or exploit to find an advantage in the battle. It is critical to maintain holiness and personal purity in the battle offensive. Believers must not let preaching or service or study crowd out prayer life, times of devotion, praise, or time in the Word. The Word is the key to all that is dear to the body of Christ. These things are the line of supply to be effective in the battle that the Lord has called forth. They will give fuel for the battle.

Our enemy is no fool; he is very clever. He has been at this warfare thing for eons longer than current believers have been alive. He is battle hardened. The enemy will try to stretch our lines until we cannot hold it. The more intense the battle, the more that people must pray. The enemy will try to exploit the line at a decisive point. The devil will look for the weak spots. He knows what they are and that is where he will hit the hardest. He will not hit until he thinks that he can crack the will of the people he attacks. Jesus fasted, and Satan was ineffective in derailing the kingdom plan by derailing Jesus. After Satan could not distract Jesus from his God-given purposes, he departed until he could regroup, and try to come at Jesus during a time of weakness. The book of Luke gives one of Satan's prime strategies: "Now when the devil had ended *every* temptation, *he departed from Him until an opportune time*" (Luke 4:13). If the enemy cannot trip us up, he will depart until a more opportune time. Our battle strategy must be to not give him a more opportune time by keeping our sword (the Word) sharp and our relationship close to the Lord.

To be effective on the offensive, there are some things to keep in mind:

- Know the enemy. As much as possible believers must know his objectives and strategies. The Lord will give divine revelation through communion with him and by staying in the Word of God. Believers must know what Satan is after and must know what God is after. In other words, the objectives of both teams are clearly defined and must be understood.
- Do not engage in unnecessary battles, but only those things which point to the immediate or ultimate objective of the manifestation of the kingdom of God on the earth as it is in heaven.
- Do not become passive in the battle. This is true even if believers have a temporary advantage. As seen with the example of the ballgame above, to be ahead and then let up often leads to defeat!
- Do not lose the will to fight. There is an ultimate kingdom plan. When Christians maintain relationship with the Lord and his supply, there is strength for the battle. Having said that, it is important to recognize that as human beings rest is necessary. However, it appears from Scripture that Jesus' times of rest were resting in the Father. Believers are renewed in the presence of God, much more than on a beach with a good novel or fishing.
- Remember that the enemy will strike at the weakest point. He will not hit until there are weaknesses, and then he

will hit hard. Therefore, believers must be proactive about knowing their own weaknesses and bringing self-exposure. When I have sinned, the first thing that I have learned to do is to go quickly to my husband to confess and allow him to hold me accountable. By bringing my weaknesses out into the open, my weaknesses are weakened. (That is a double negative, which is a positive.) In other words, by weakening my weaknesses, I allow myself to become stronger in the Lord. The sin that will ultimately hurt is the one that remains hidden. Exposed sin soon loses its power to destroy.

In every battle there is a decisive point. There is a point where the end is determined but not yet secured. There is a point that the possession of which will allow an army to achieve victory or to be defeated. Prayer is the decisive point of spiritual battles. Praise is the weapon that stuns and renders the enemy ineffective in his battle plan. Fasting is a tool that is not in favor, but is very powerful and effective in rendering the enemy severely weakened in the battle. Believers must pray and not faint. If believers do not pray, weak spots will become vulnerable spots. Remember that a battle offensive in prayer is an attitude and an action. Develop an attitude of being aggressive in prayer with the action of taking ground. We are called to be offensive, but with wisdom and caution.

Chapter 12

Cooperation

Cooperation is the process of working together toward an appointed goal. Joseph Carroll said that the idea of cooperation in a military endeavor depends on two prerequisites: First, that the parties cooperating are allies and not combatants, and second, that they come under one commander.[23] Those requirements would be good in any collaborative situation.

It can be said without reservation that those in cooperation must be allies. However, in the Church, those who should be our apparent allies are often not our allies at all. There are many denominational differences and separations within the body of Christ. The Lord is not coming for a broken bride of many factions who cannot be in agreement with each other. The book of Revelation says, "Let us be glad and rejoice and give Him glory, for the marriage of the Lamb has come, and *His wife has made herself ready*" (Rev. 19:7). The Lord is coming for a bride who has made herself ready to meet her groom as a spotless and pure bride. He is coming for one bride, not many brides.

The lack of cooperation within the body is one reason that the body of Christ is weak in the battle against our enemy. Because the body of Christ is fighting against itself, it cannot mount an attack against the kingdom of darkness. The book of Matthew says, "Every kingdom divided against itself is brought to desolation, and

---

[23] See previous footnote about Joseph Carroll.

every city or house divided against itself will not stand" (Matt. 12:25). The word *desolation* means "to lay waste to." That is what is happening to the body because we have forgotten that the enemy is Satan, and not our brothers and sisters who may worship under a different sign on the door. The body of Christ is laid waste because of infighting in senseless and petty disputes that play right into Satan's hand.

The Priestly Prayer of Jesus in the garden of Gethsemane illustrates his concern that the body of Christ be unified:

> "I do not pray for these alone, but also for those who will believe in Me through their word; that they all may be one, as You, Father, *are* in Me, and I in You; that they also may be one in Us, *that the world may believe that You sent Me*. And the glory which You gave Me I have given them, that they may be one just as We are one: I in them, and You in Me; that they may be made perfect in one, and *that the world may know that You have sent Me*, and have loved them as You have loved Me. (John 17:20-23)

Unfortunately, the body of Christ tramples on the image of Christ in the world every time that believers are not in one accord. We trample on Jesus' name and image because he said that as believers are made perfect as one, the world would know that the Father sent the Son. The world does not know that the Son is from the Father because of the petty differences that keep the body of believers separated.

Joseph Carroll's second requirement for cooperation was that the forces be united under one headship or under one commander. That is fine and good until egos are running wide open and everyone wants to be the top dog. The Lord will establish leadership and usually it comes with a high cost. Where there is not one person who is in charge, there are times when leaders of equal rank come to an impasse. However, where clear leadership lines are drawn, and where cooperation exists, the potential for exponential use of force against the enemy is realized: "And five of you shall chase a hundred, and a hundred of you shall put ten thousand to flight: and your enemies shall fall before you by the sword" (Lev. 26:8). In unity and cooperation, the power and force that can be mounted against the enemy is exponential!

Cooperation demands that egos take a back seat to the greater good of the whole. In actuality, there will be many apostolic leaders in the days ahead who will lead the Church, but they must submit in humble servanthood even though they are leaders. In a military war, for example, there may be many generals, but even generals of tens of thousands of troops do not act independently. Even the generals are subject to the overarching strategy of the commander in chief. True apostolic leaders yield to the ministry and guidance of the Holy Spirit and to accountability of other leaders. Even apostles should have leadership over them, usually other apostolic leaders that they have submitted themselves to in a mentoring or accountability relationship.

The level of cooperation is put to the test in hard battles. The level of cooperation is challenged when there is more than one person who wants to be in charge, or more than one person who thinks that they know what is the best thing to do in any situation. The Lord will say who has the ultimate say. It is the Spirit of God, of course, but he will select a chosen person to be the leader over any fighting contingency. There was not usually a committee to make decisions in Scripture, although there were a few council meetings along the way (See Acts 15, for example). Councils cannot lead on a battlefield. Councils set policy, but battles demand the leadership of a general, a strong and firm voice who will lead the troops into battle!

The closer the commander is to the cooperative forces, the closer the cooperation. That is why leaders should keep a close eye on everything that is happening around them and under their leadership. Cooperation leads to concentration on the given objective. In a situation where there is a lack of cooperation, the attention is often given to those who should be our allies and not to the ultimate objective. What is necessary is that believers and leaders "Keep their eyes on the ball!" Effective leaders keep their eyes open so they can stop the efforts of the enemy to divide cooperation.

If a leader cannot keep watch, he or she needs to delegate those under their leadership to keep an eye on things that are happening around them. The closer the commander is to the situation or field of battle, the more he can enforce cooperation. The commander needs to keep a close tab so he can deal with elements that would hinder cooperation.

Many Christian leaders like to work on an individual basis. However, the Lord set up leadership structures in the Word. There were leadership structures in the Old Testament, and there were different leadership structures in the New Testament. When people are in their assigned positions that the Lord has ordained, there will be no jockeying for position. Cooperation of the body of Christ has to be on the terms of the Holy Spirit through the chosen and established leadership. There are times that it appears that people want help to fulfill *their plan*, not to see what God is doing in the plans of others. It could be said that we live in a selfish age which promotes individualism. Many people are promoting their own personal ministries but are not promoting the kingdom of God. The more an ego needs to be fed, the bigger it gets. The bigger it gets, the more it wants to be fed. Never feed the ego; it is a slippery slope that believers and leaders do not want to go down.

When the body of believers can put aside personal gain, and promote God's kingdom, cooperation will come in a way that glorifies God and lets the world know that the Father sent the Son. This is what cooperation in the body can do. The book of Matthew says, "Again I say to you that if two of you agree on earth concerning anything that they ask, it will be done for them by My Father in heaven. For where two or three are gathered together in My name, I am there in the midst of them" (Matt. 18:19-20). There is tremendous power in true cooperation and when the body of Christ is in one accord.

The current generation has never seen true unity in the body of Christ. Before the Lord can do what he wants to do, there will have to be

Our generation has never seen true unity in the body of Christ. Before the Lord can do what he wants to do, there will have to be true unity.

true unity. Prima donnas or heroes are not needed in the kingdom realm. The call is to go lower and let the team go higher as a unit. If one seeks glory here on the earth, they have all the glory they will ever receive. There is no place for stars in God's kingdom. In sporting events, heroes are usually a hindrance and not a help. The Lord had a team. He trained them. There is an element of sacrifice in God's kingdom that is not seen in the world. Jesus was the greatest example of a sacrificing servant. There is sacrifice in true cooperation. In authentic cooperation there is a willingness to sacrifice self for others and for the sake of the cause. In true cooperation, believers will learn to subjugate their individual desires for the good of others. That is when the army of Christ will truly be a factor to route and destroy the works of the devil. One of Jesus' purposes on earth was to destroy the works of the devil, and he left believers on the planet to bring to fullness what he already completed.

Fostering cooperation is a gift that some people have, but all leaders need to foster cooperation to get people to work together just as the Father, Son, and Holy Spirit evidenced in the Word of God. Leaders must maintain unity in order to achieve the objective. Believers should not fight each other. They must fight together so that the kingdom objectives of God may be achieved. There is a call for believers to deny themselves to obtain the objectives of God. Each member of the body is a part of a team. Paul, the greatest apostle of the New Testament says:

> And those members of the body which we think to be less honorable, on these we *bestow greater honor*; and our unpresentable parts have greater modesty, but our presentable parts have no need. But God composed the body, *having given greater honor to that part which lacks it,* that there should be no schism in the body, but that the members should have the same care for one another. (1 Cor. 12:23-25)

Humanity sets the hierarchy of the structure of leadership. God does not make one higher than the other. Some are called to be leaders, but in God's eyes, leaders do not have more honor than the one who cleans the latrine. All are valuable in the kingdom realm. There is a sense of belonging in the army of God. A strong individualist ruins team spirit. Team spirit of cooperation means sacrificing personal opinions, desires, and self-will for achieving the objective for the good of the team. There is only one commander, which is ultimately the Holy Spirit. The Spirit of God selects and empowers the leaders that he has chosen. When there is one command, there is no disunity. A divided command leads to loss. There is a call to obey one commander. Even leaders have to be under the absolute leadership of the Spirit of God to follow where he is leading.

This spirit of cooperation is evident in the Godhead. Each one holds up the other parts of the Trinity in Scripture. The Father holds up the Son: "This is My beloved Son, in whom I am well pleased. Hear Him!" (Matt. 17:50). The Son holds up the Father: "Most assuredly, I say to you, the Son can do nothing of Himself, but what He sees the Father do; for whatever He does, the Son also does in like manner" (John 5:19), and "You have heard Me say to you, ... 'I am going to the Father,' for My Father is greater than I" (John 14:28). The Father gave the gift of the Holy Spirit by the testimony of the Son: "And being assembled together with them, He commanded them not to depart from Jerusalem, but to wait for the Promise of the Father, 'Which,' He said, 'you have heard from Me; for John truly baptized with water, but you shall be baptized with the Holy Spirit not many days from now'" (Acts 1:4-5). The Spirit points to the Son: "But the Helper, the Holy Spirit, whom the Father will send in My name, He will teach you all things, and bring to your remembrance all things that I said to you" (John 14:26). The Spirit was poured out by the Father: "And it shall come to pass afterward That I will pour out My Spirit on all flesh; Your sons and your daughters shall prophesy, your old men shall dream dreams, your young men shall see visions. And also on My menservants and on My maidservants I will pour out My Spirit in those days" (Joel 2:28-29). The Holy Trinity demonstrated a complete lack of self-serving attitudes as each part points to and glorifies the other parts. The Godhead is one God demonstrated and manifested in three ways. That should be our image of the unity of the Church.

There is a synergy in the connection of leaders as they cooperate. The synergy is greater than the sum of the parts. Unity is a huge part of synergy. Synergy is the interaction or cooperation of two or more things working together to produce a combined effect that is greater than the sum of their individual parts. Synergy is truly a kingdom concept. Synergy is a function of kingdom multiplication. Likewise, that is what marriage is in the kingdom of God. It is joining as the Lord joins with his believers. The people are greater than they could be if not joined with him. That means that the "person" part of the relationship is greater by joining with the Lord than each person could be on his or her own. The Lord transforms people when they join with him. It is not the sum of the parts. It is not addition; it is multiplication. In fact, joining with the Lord is exponential multiplication. Believers are multiplied when they are in relationship with the Lord and other believers. Everyone is multiplied in deep relationship with the Lord. We can do more as the Lord's extension than we ever could under our own power.

One Accord

Apostolic leaders should lead their teams toward building unity in God's camp while destroying unity in Satan's camp. When unity exists, it is incredible what can happen within the body of believers. The five-fold ministry is an integral part of leadership, consisting of apostles, prophets, evangelists, pastors and teachers. The end result of the establishment of the five-fold ministry is unity. These classes of leaders are often discussed in ministry settings, but it is rare to hear that the ultimate goal of their assignment is unity. The ultimate goal of the leadership structure of the New Testament is to equip believers for works of ministry, to edify or build up the body, *until there is unity* (Eph. 4:13).

Equipping and edifying are the ways to get to the end result of unity. The very purpose of the leadership structure is to create an atmosphere where the same passions control the body as a whole. Those passions may include the will of God to see Jesus enthroned as the King of kings and the manifestation of God's kingdom on the earth. The importance of unity in the leadership structure of

Ephesians 4 for building the kingdom of God cannot be overstated. The full context of Ephesians says,

> And He Himself gave some to be apostles, some prophets, some evangelists, and some pastors and teachers, for the equipping of the saints for the work of ministry, for the edifying of the body of Christ, *till we all come to the unity of the faith and of the knowledge of the Son of God*, to a perfect man, to the measure of the stature of the fullness of Christ; that we should no longer be children, tossed to and fro and carried about with every wind of doctrine, by the trickery of men, in the cunning craftiness of deceitful plotting, but, speaking the truth in love, may grow up in all things into Him who is the head—Christ—from whom the whole body, *joined and knit together by what every joint supplies*, according to the effective working by *which every part does its share*, causes growth of the body for the edifying of itself in love. (Eph. 4:11-16)

Victory often comes when people are brought together by a common vision. That is what has happened often in Scripture and in history. It is not just that the people are in one accord, they are in one accord toward a common goal. The book of Acts also highlights that they were in one accord in one place.

In a military setting, it is easy to have a common goal during wartime. The goal is simple: Defeat the enemy! It may not be so easy to get the branches of military focused on a common cause where there is no real threat that must be dealt with. In peacetime, unity may be more difficult. The same is true in the body of believers. Where there is a situation that causes grave concern, it may be easy to unify the troops toward a common vision. We have arrived to the place of grave concern in the world. This is the time, like never before, to be unified toward a common vision of enthroning the King of kings on the earth and dethroning the enemy.

Going forward, the job of the apostolic and other leaders is to unite people toward a common vision to effectuate the change that is needed. The first objective is to ascertain what that vision is according to the will of God, and the second objective is to convey it to the people so that they can understand the ultimate objective so that all may be unified. Common vision minimizes confusion and brings something to be unified about. Each apostolic leader chosen by God has strengths and weaknesses. The more united that each leader is to God's vision for the Church, the more united is the total call of the body of Christ. As people seek the will of God for his kingdom, common vision will begin to emerge. God has an overarching objective and when people work toward the implementation of that objective, unity will come. There is a lot of work to be done, but the apostolic leadership of Jesus by the power of the Holy Spirit will guide to that end.

Chapter 13

God's Network Plan

Before a few years ago, I hardly knew anyone outside of my home state of Kentucky. Since that time there has been an explosion of connections that my husband and I have made around the nation and across the world. We have friends and ministry partners all over the country and literally from many nations. We have had people who have come to us and stayed in our home; we have gone to them and been their guests. The global impact of the connections has been mind boggling. We have met so many people, only to come to learn that the people we have met know other people we know. There always seems to be some level of connection.

As we have connected with the leaders and believers from around the world, we talk about what the Lord is doing. The connections are incredible and almost seem to be emerging without any real effort to create those connections. In other words, the connections are not contrived; they have just unfolded. This seems to be something that is happening throughout the body of believers. The Lord seems to be building a network plan to connect his body to one another. It is very exciting to see what the Lord is going to do from this point forward.

How do apostolic leaders build unity? Some apostles are world-class networkers. When the leadership is walking in humility and yieldedness, that means that no one is trying to build a personal kingdom. When people are not building personal kingdoms, they are interested in building God's kingdom. The outcome is that they are humble in seeking to hold others up.

Many biblical leaders were great networkers. The original apostles had a great network in an age without cell phones, computers, or jets. They were networked, and they created a system of communication that allowed them to stay informed. They all worked toward the common goal and vision. The book of Acts is filled with accounts of the teamwork and unity (along with some discord, too) across vast distances at the time. Paul was a great sender of both people and information. He managed to maintain connection with those people he sent to other locations and with those churches, leaders, and believers to which he gave apostolic oversight. He was a great communicator. When he sent letters of encouragement, they were shared with all the churches in the region. In fact, two-thirds of the New Testament resulted from Paul's endless efforts to stay connected with those to whom he was providing apostolic oversight.

The apostles maintained a strong connection with the Jerusalem church, the home base of all of the ministries. Paul was a networker, and he was connected with other apostles who had their own networks. Even the networks were networked. He collected offerings from the outlying churches to send to Jerusalem. It was often mentioned in Acts that Paul would try to get back to Jerusalem for the feasts and holy days. He was connected to about every other New Testament ministry that is mentioned in Acts. He was a builder and a networker. He was also tough as nails when others were not doing what they should be doing. He called out Peter publically for slacking on receiving Gentile believers with the openness that the Lord demanded: "Now when Peter had come to Antioch, I (Paul) withstood him to his face, because he was to be blamed" (Gal. 2:11, See 2:11-14). Leaders are not concerned about personal popularity, which is really the fear of men, but are more concerned with the fear of God.

Networking is paramount to the apostolic call for the last days. Believers are going to need the connection and support with believers at home and around the world. Apostolic leaders of this age will need to be great networkers as well. There is strength in working together. Many are already working in networks. As leaders build networks, their networks will build networks until the globe is covered.

Partnership

Partnership with others was seen even in the opening scenes of the New Testament. As Jesus called his first disciples, they had toiled all night, catching no fish. Jesus told them to go out into the deep and let down the nets. When Peter followed the Lord's plan, the catch was so great that they could not bring in the harvest. They called

Because they were already in a partnership relationship, they were able to move into action immediately when the need came.

their associates in the other boat to bring in reinforcements. The book of Luke says, "So they *signaled to their partners in the other boat to come and help them.* And they came and filled both the boats, so that they began to sink" (Luke 5:7). Peter was not selfish with the catch by trying to hoard it all for himself. He called his partners when the nets began to break so the harvest would not be lost. His partners were James and John, the sons of Zebedee. Jesus said to Simon, "Do not be afraid. From now on you will catch men" (Luke 5:10). These men were partners before Jesus called them, and they continued to be partners after Jesus called them.

There are a few things to consider in this passage. First, they had partners. They were not lone wolves, so to speak. They worked in tandem with others for a common purpose. Second, the partners were strategic. They were in place when the need arose for them to come to the rescue. They shared the labor; they shared the harvest. Third, the partnership was already established before the crisis of the overflow hit. Because they were already in partnership relationship, they were able to move into action immediately when the need came. They did not have a courtship or a contract to establish the boundaries of the division of the catch that had to be hammered out right then; they had already done that long ago.

Finally, they were in close proximity to each other. They did not have to send across the land to try to get reinforcements. The partners were with them in the area. If the partners had not been close, the harvest would have been lost. The nets were already breaking, so quick action was necessary.

I recently heard a story of a pastor who experienced a tremendous revival in his church. There was an explosion of young people coming to his church. He continued the revival meeting to gather the fish in the net. However, when he came to the fullness of his capacity to manage the harvest, he called in reinforcements. When he came to the point that he could not adequately disciple the young believers, he called another pastor in his area and told him that he was sending about 200 people to his church. When the first pastor was asked why he would do such a thing, he answered, "Because the Lord told me to build ministry in my city, not in my church." That is kingdom growth, and not personal growth. How many are willing to give up a harvest that they cannot hold on to anyway, and bless someone else's ministry? Kingdom leaders are willing to do just that because they are building God's kingdom and not their own kingdoms.

Paul also made a couple of mentions of partnership. He said, "If anyone inquires about Titus, *he is my partner and fellow worker concerning you*. Or if our brethren are inquired about, they are messengers of the churches, the glory of Christ" (2 Cor. 8:23). Paul also said, "If then you *count me as a partner*, receive him as you would me" (Phlm. 1:17).

Pray for strategic partners now so that the harvest is not wasted developing partnerships later when the harvest is in the nets. The Lord is clearly calling his body to be unified. It seems that there is going to be a greater connectivity among the body of believers. The language will be restored so that there is unity. There is one bride of Christ that will be pure and ready. That means that all historical divisions within the Church will be mended. The body of Christ will be as a seamless cloth.

It seems that before there can be unity in all things, there must be connection. How can we be unified with believers that we do not know and do not understand what they believe? Does the connection come before the unity? The connection comes from believers and leaders being networked together. Before things can be united, they have to be connected. A person cannot be in one accord with someone with which they have no connection. The book of Ecclesiastes supports the idea that believers are not supposed to be singular in the walk of faith.

> Two are better than one, because they have a good reward for their labor. For if they fall, one will lift up his companion. But woe to him who is alone when he falls, for he has no one to help him up. Again, if two lie down together, they will keep warm; But how can one be warm alone? Though one may be overpowered by another, two can withstand him. And a threefold cord is not quickly broken. (Eccles. 4:9-12)

The Bible supports that there is strength in numbers. Especially in the days ahead, the body will need the strength of the support of others. The book of Hebrews shares how believers encourage and press others in the faith. It says, "Let us consider how we may spur one another on toward love and good deeds. Let us not give up meeting together, as some are in the habit of doing, but let us encourage one another—and all the more as you see the day approaching" (Heb. 10:24-25).

Paul also said, "Now I plead with you, brethren, by the name of our Lord Jesus Christ, that you all speak the same thing, and *that there be no divisions among you, but that you be perfectly joined together in the same mind and in the same judgment*" (1 Cor. 1:10). Paul was asking the church to make sure that there were no divisions among them. There could be no divisions if there was no connection in the first place. This passage is calling for perfect unity among them. Perfect unity means to be in one accord in mind and judgment. Perfect unity requires connection. Furthermore, simply being connected does not necessarily mean that the connected parts are unified. But before things can be unified, they have to be connected.

The relevance of the five-fold ministry passage is emerging as has been mentioned. Paul wrote that the end goal of leadership is to, *"Come to the unity of the faith and of the knowledge of the Son of God"* (Eph. 4:13). The end goal of this passage was to create unity, but the preceding instructions are to equip and edify. This is a call to build up the body until there is unity. The unity is in the faith and in the knowledge of the Son of God. Did you catch that? The unity is for the purpose of coming to faith and the knowledge of God! The whole purpose of the five-fold ministry is culminated in that one sentence: Primarily to bring people to the knowledge of God. When the body of Christ is unified, the strategy of knowledge will be fully known by the body. This means that the defeated enemy will be broken and his yoke will be removed from the earth. Unity leads to knowledge and strategy, which leads to victory!

Networking individual members, Paul also said, "Bearing with one another, and forgiving one another, if anyone has a complaint against another; even as Christ forgave you, so you also must do. But above all these things put on love, which is the bond of perfection" (Col. 3:13-14). This passage encompasses the two concepts: connection and unity. Paul talked about bearing with others which means, "to hold up, endure, or to put up with." The bond of unity means, "being tied together." How do we bear with each other if we are not connected in the first place? Bear with each other and then be bonded in unity. Networking is to hold others in connection until maturity comes.

In the upper room on the day of Pentecost, there were 120 people who were connected. The people in Jerusalem for Pentecost were from all over the world. When the Holy Spirit came, they were restored to unity and connection in the language. Acts 2 gave a rundown on who was present:

> And how is it that we hear, each in our own language in which we were born? Parthians and Medes and Elamites, those dwelling in Mesopotamia, Judea and Cappadocia, Pontus and Asia, Phrygia and Pamphylia, Egypt and the parts of Libya adjoining Cyrene, visitors from Rome, both Jews

and proselytes, Cretans and Arabs—we hear them
speaking in our own tongues the wonderful works
of God." So they were all amazed and perplexed,
saying to one another, "Whatever could this mean?"
(Acts 2:9-12)

They were from many lands, cultures, and with many languages. They were connected by the Spirit of God in a way that
they could never have been connected under their own devices.
They were also in "one place" which seems to be important on the
day of Pentecost. They were in one accord because they, among
other things, were together in one place. In many ways this was a
reversal of the separation of Genesis 11, when God confused the
language.

The tower of Babel is actually a reverse networking situation.
In Genesis 11, the people were networking against God and he
scattered them, which was just what they were trying to avoid in
the first place. They said, "Let us make a name for ourselves, *lest
we be scattered abroad over the face of the whole earth.*" ... And
the LORD said, "Indeed the people are one and they all have one
language, and this is what they begin to do*; now nothing that they
propose to do will be withheld from them.*" (Gen. 11:4,6). They
built the tower in their pride, and in their foolish self-interest, they
tried to reach God through their own achievement. In the unity of
their language nothing was impossible for them. They suffered
division because of their arrogance. The world was divided into
many languages and cultures, and the divisions became common-
place. This should speak to modern believers and leaders about the
need to cultivate and foster humility.

The author of the book of Acts, however, observed God doing
something radically different. In the midst of the division in the
world, the church was gathered, "They were all together in one
place" (Acts 2:1). They were all filled with God's Spirit and began
to speak in "other languages." The languages, unlike the ones from
the Babel story, did not create division. Actually, the opposite effect
happened when the bewildered crowd came together because each
one heard in his or her own language. It was not yet a state of unity

of having a pure language, but it was a start toward a perfect unity. The book of Zephaniah says, "For then I will restore to the peoples a pure language, that they all may call on the name of the LORD, to serve Him with one accord" (Zeph. 3:9). God said out of his own mouth, in Genesis 11, that nothing would be impossible for them when their language was united. That principle holds true for the Church as well. When the body of believers is unified in Christ Jesus, there is nothing that will be impossible.

Currently, even the Church has become accustomed to the divisions. In fact, a divided Church with no unity is all that current believers have ever known. Believers in this age have never lived in a time when there were no denominations and even denominational sub-parts, all broken over doctrinal differences. Scripture reveals that apostles are the ones to establish doctrine. When the Church gave up on the five-fold ministry and being dedicated to the apostles' teaching, divisions came. Going back to the beginning of the Church in Acts, to the times of apostles' listening to the Lord and establishing doctrine, unity will be restored. In the days and times ahead, God seems to be up to something to bring unity back to the body of believers. Apostolic leaders may be called into the arena of networking. That may mean building a network and networking those networks with other networks. Discerning apostolic leaders must tune in to hear what is happening in the spirit realm and with the Holy Spirit to create unity in the body of Christ.

Chapter 14

Intelligence

In any military endeavor, the collection of information in the form of intelligence of the enemy is a factor that can change the course of the battle or even the war. Countries invest untold resources in knowing what those around them know and what they are doing. Knowing one's enemy can be decisive in war. In spiritual warfare, intelligence comes from the Holy Spirit. In fact, Holy Spirit intelligence is what the first part of this book is about. Believers will have all the intelligence that is needed when they listen to the Lord and hear what the Spirit would say about ongoing military operations and situations involving the enemy.

The Holy Spirit will telegraph what the enemy is doing when we pause to listen and hear his intelligence reports. Believers must never entertain anything but the thought of absolute victory. It is ours in Jesus Christ. We do not look at the natural; we look at the supernatural, saying "Victory is ours!" We are not frightened by the enemy. In the Holy Spirit, we seek continual protection against the enemy.

Believers must realize that there will be a "final stand" against the enemy. That is the final battle just before the enemy caves in and surrenders. There may be many fierce battles where the enemy is turned back, but even so, the enemy will put up one final battle in the last stand. There will be some very decisive battles in the spiritual walk. There will be many small battles, but the decisive battles must be won.

Many people will have big individual battles that they face to establish the call that God has on their lives. The enemy will fight hard against God's chosen ones. Most usually, those who are chosen have to fight to hold on the call that the Lord has given them. The enemy will try to wrest it out of their hands and defeat God's purposes for those who have been called. If a person loses that primary battle for the calling and purpose, the defeat could change the person's ability to meet the destiny and purpose that God has for his or her life. A defeat in personal battle of a great magnitude may mean that the person will lose or be delayed in their ability to be a factor as a warrior in the spiritual realm. The Spirit will help believers win any battle that is faced. However, it is imperative that the person seek the intelligence that the Spirit of God knows so that there can be release of strategy to have the victory. Perhaps even more important, is that the will of a person not be defeated amidst great trials and personal hardships. Overcoming and being victorious in those battles forms character and reveals anointing. Most people who are generals in God's army have battle scars to show for the anointing that they carry.

When the Spirit gives intelligence of the enemy, who he is, and who are his allies, the victory will be easier to obtain. There was much Holy Spirit intelligence in Scripture. One prime example of Holy Spirit intelligence is found in 2 Kings:

> Now the king of Syria was making war against Israel; and he consulted with his servants, saying, "My camp will be in such and such a place." And the man of God sent to the king of Israel, saying, "Beware that you do not pass this place, for the Syrians are coming down there." Then the king of Israel sent someone to the place of which the man of God had told him. Thus he warned him, and he was watchful there, *not just once or twice*. Therefore, *the heart of the king of Syria was greatly troubled by this thing;* and he called his servants and said to

them, *"Will you not show me which of us is for the king of Israel?"* And one of his servants said, "None, my lord, O king; *but Elisha, the prophet who is in Israel, tells the king of Israel the words that you speak in your bedroom."* (2 Kings 6:8-12)

The prophet Elisha told the king of Israel what the king of Syria was saying in his private chamber. The Syrian king wanted to know who the spy was in his midst. He could not figure out how the opposing king knew his moves before he made them. The prophet Elisha was talking to a spy who was on a recognizance mission. He was receiving intelligence reports from the Holy Spirit. If God did it then for a prophet who was forecasting what a pagan king was doing, he will do it now with our enemy, Satan.

We must ask ourselves, what are Satan's intentions and what is he after? What are his objectives? Satan follows the principles of war. He will concentrate his forces at the weakest point every time without fail. His intelligence team is very efficient. If we know his methods of operating, believers have an advantage. The same is true if we know his strategy. How does he achieve his objectives? In physical warfare, intelligence officers will try to crack the secret codes of the enemy. In spiritual warfare, believers can easily have the code in the intelligence information given by the Holy Spirit.

We do not have to be ignorant of the devices of the enemy. We have the availability to know what he is doing. With the alertness of the Holy Spirit, we can know the enemy and the battles that he will bring our way well in advance of the battle lines being drawn.

Knowledge about what the enemy is saying lets us counter it efficiently. Praise and worship jams the enemy's communications. Know his methods of operating and jam them. Believers should know warfare tactics that overcome the warfare tactics that the enemy uses to distract the body of believers.

Joseph Carroll says recognize, refuse, and resist the ploys of the enemy. It is important to *recognize* the ploys of the enemy. Peter said to the Lord that Jesus would never die. Jesus recognized the plan of Satan in Peter's words and said for Satan to get behind him (Matt. 16:23). Believers can overcome the enemy by *refusing* to take what he is offering. The body of believers must also *resist* Satan's advances by actively going after God: "Therefore submit to God. Resist the devil and he will flee from you" (James 4:7). When the believers recognize, refuse, and resist, then they will be released.[24]

Believers will fight some crucial battles. The outcome depends on if individuals are really in the place where God wants them to be and if they are at the right place at the right time. The outcome depends on how close we are to the Lord and if we have the vital intelligence that we need to overcome the battle plans of the enemy. We do not have to be ignorant of the devices of the enemy. We have the availability to know what he is doing. With the alertness of the Holy Spirit, we can know the enemy and the battles that he will bring our way well in advance of the battle lines being drawn.

Believers and leaders, in particular, must have the mind of the Holy Spirit to discern the greatest enemies. Sometimes those are the enemies that are even within the camp. The Holy Spirit will give knowledge and discernment of those who are in the midst that are not trustworthy. Knowing the enemy includes knowing the enemy that is within, as much as knowing the enemy that is without. There is usually at least one Judas in any fellowship. It is important to know that there may be people within your midst who are not trustworthy. Know who the Judas' are within your fellowship. Who are the traitors? Who are the wolves in sheep's clothing? Judas was in the most-trusted position because he had the money bag, but he was the biggest thief of all.

Who is the greatest enemy? It is Satan, of course, but he also enlists the help of allies. He is very efficient and experienced. He has been at this attempt to defeat God's people and God's plan for thousands of years. The enemy's camp knows how to be strategic. If believers want to fight him without the Holy Spirit, we fight in vain. His allies are sharks: The enemies within. The enemies without are the world and his demonic forces. He uses the

---

[24] See previous footnote about Joseph Carroll.

combination of both enemies to defeat God's people. There are very harsh forces waiting to ambush believers who are not listening to the intelligence reports. Know the enemies that war against the Church. The enemy knows how to manipulate those who are enemies within the camp. Believers must know the enemies who know Satan. We must know his allies, too.

Chapter 15

Line of Supply

Napoléon Bonaparte once said, "An army marches on its stomach." In order for the troops to be good soldiers, they must have all of the supplies they need. The supply line of the army is critical for the outcome, not only of specific battles but of the entire war. If an army does not maintain supplies, they will have to surrender to the enemy. Even a superior force will be rendered helpless if it is not supplied with food, medical stores, or even ammunition. Guns without bullets are powerless, no matter how well the troops are trained. Even the magnificently trained Navy Seals or Green Berets will be rendered ineffective if they do not have the munitions or gear to which they have become accustomed. They are extremely effective forces, but they are also probably the best supplied units in the entire military.

The enemy will try to cut the supply line and keep it cut to strangle the army. Those who are equipped fight the battle on their own terms. The outcome of the war depends on the entire supply. In the army of God, all that we need to live comes from union with Christ. The only source believers need is Jesus Christ. What do we need to function here on earth as victorious Christians? We have the victory, but how do we appropriate the power of Jesus Christ as the victory on the earth in a fallen world? In Christ are hidden all the treasures of wisdom and knowledge:

That the God of our Lord Jesus Christ, the Father
of glory, may give to you the spirit of wisdom and
revelation in the knowledge of Him, the eyes of
your understanding being enlightened; that you may
know what is the hope of His calling, what are the
riches of the glory of His inheritance in the saints,
and what is the exceeding greatness of His power
toward us who believe, according to the working
of His mighty power which He worked in Christ
when He raised Him from the dead and seated Him
at His right hand in the heavenly places, far above
all principality and power and might and dominion,
and every name that is named, not only in this age
but also in that which is to come. (Eph. 1:17-22)

In Christ dwells all the fullness of the Godhead. He is the vine;
we are the branch. The vine supplies the branch:

Abide in Me, and I in you. As the branch cannot
bear fruit of itself, unless it abides in the vine, neither can you, unless you abide in Me. "I am the
vine; you are the branches. He who abides in Me,
and I in him, bears much fruit; for without Me you
can do nothing. If anyone does not abide in Me, he
is cast out as a branch and is withered; and they
gather them and throw them into the fire, and they
are burned. If you abide in Me, and My words abide
in you, you will ask what you desire, and it shall be
done for you. (John 15:4-7)

All we need is in him. Humanity is not the source of the supply.
We are but the soldiers, but Jesus is the only source of supply. The
supply consists of the physical, emotional, and spiritual needs of
the army. He is the supply of food and ammunition, both physical
and spiritual. We can store up nothing. We have no power other
than what he supplies to us for our needs in the battle and the war.
In him alone, we are more usable and can be honed into a sharper

more effective instrument. God uses humanity, but humanity does not use him.

The enemy wants to cut the supply line or keep people thinking that there is some other source of supply. The branch makes no contribution to the life of the vine. The branch is the receiver of all supply.

The enemy wants to cut the supply line or keep people thinking that there is some other source of supply. The branch makes no contribution to the life of the vine. The branch is the receiver of all supply. The branch is the place where the fruit grows and is supplied, but only because it receives the supply from the vine first. A branch without supply of the vine soon withers and is unfruitful. Unfruitful branches are cut off and thrown into the fire. They are unfruitful because they receive no supply from the vine: "Every branch in Me that does not bear fruit He takes away; and every branch that bears fruit He prunes, that it may bear more fruit.... If anyone does not abide in Me, he is cast out as a branch and is withered; and they gather them and throw them into the fire, and they are burned" (John 15:2,6).

Believers can never graduate from total, unceasing dependence on Jesus. The devil will make people think that they have amazing experiences, intellect, or other gifts. Those things are not the supply. Those things are only tools that make us more useful as an instrument in God's hands. Gifts are not the same things as supply; they are the tools to use the supply. Believers should appropriate Jesus Christ for every need. Abiding is critical; all is from Christ.

The supply comes from relationship and from staying in the Word! All Scripture is profitable for overcoming the enemy and for building a relationship with Jesus. Knowledge, wisdom, and power all are in Christ. All wisdom, all knowledge, and all power belong to him: "There shall come forth a Rod from the stem of Jesse, and a Branch shall grow out of his roots. The Spirit of the Lord shall rest upon Him, The Spirit of wisdom and understanding, The Spirit of counsel and might, The Spirit of knowledge and of the fear of the Lord" (Isa. 11:1-2). Believers only get the supply needed from being in him! Revelation comes through Christ by the Holy Spirit.

The devil will seek to deceive and misdirect to say that which a person needs is from some source other than the Living Christ who is in us by his Spirit. Jesus is the sole source.

We have a lot of equipment and resources, but it takes power to set that machinery in motion. Jesus Christ is everything! Very few realize this, even among the body of believers. Very few people live by this understanding. That is why very few people live as victorious Christians. All the enemy has to do is cut the supply line, and soon the vine begins to wither. Suddenly, the believer stops bearing fruit. Some "Christians" may be barren or have a lot of foliage or apparent growth with no fruit at all. Many people in the body have never born any fruit for God's kingdom. The Word tells us that unfruitful branches will be cut away and thrown into the fire.

Often the most *unspiritual spiritual* people are the busiest, but not the most fruitful. Think of Mary and Martha, for example (Luke 10:38-42). The one who chose the better path was the one who sat at the feet of Jesus to receive teaching from the Word of the Master. Busy is not the same thing as fruitful. There are busy bees buzzing around, but they are not productive in anything that matters or which is called forth by God. The Holy Spirit will settle a person first to thrust him or her forward later. The bigger the load that the Lord wants a person to bear, the quieter that person will need to become in seeking him.

The enemy will try to give a false supply line. The most obvious one is the brain; many people rely on their intellect. It is easy to be on the right track, but then get an idea that is false and then get distracted. The supply line is vital to turning aside from that which would cause a person to be defeated. Never be turned aside from appropriating Jesus Christ for every need. Here are some rules that Joseph Carroll suggested.[25]

- Satan will try to destroy the home base, then get the believer stranded in foreign territory.
- Do not lay hands on anyone suddenly. In other words, do not ordain immature people because they will get out into deep water and before they know it, they are over their heads. It is also necessary to know the character of the

---

[25] See previous footnote about Joseph Carroll.

people that are being put into ministry settings, so that there is not an "enemy within" put into ministry who will later cause problems for the body of believers.

- To maintain the supply line a believer must not go too far too fast. Do not outrun the supply and end up with a program. Many programs are the result of having no supply from Jesus.

- A cut in the prayer line cuts the supply line. What is the counter offensive? Set aside prayer time each day and keep it. There is nothing more important. It is a vitally important appointment that must be kept. Daniel prayed three times a day, and he was greatly favored by God. Pray at least two or three times per day. Once a believer makes a commitment to pray, the devil will fight it hard. That alone is a testament to the power of prayer and keeping the communication open with the Lord.

Chapter 16

Surprise

Many of the great military coups of the past have been accomplished by the element of surprise. On Christmas night in 1776, General George Washington crossed the icy Delaware River to lead some 2,400 Continental Army troops on an unexpected raid against German Hessian mercenaries garrisoned at Trenton, New Jersey. They were a force far superior to the Continental Army in training and resources. Washington's troops caught the enemy completely off guard. The success of the Battle of Trenton raised morale of Washington's rag-tag army and proved that a more professional army could be outwitted by a weaker fighting force. The element of surprise was a huge factor. Being alert to the possibility of surprise is a point that will keep any army on its toes.

The Japanese attack on Pearl Harbor in 1941 was a tremendous victory for Japan because a huge part of the U.S. naval fleet was docked in the harbor and the strategists were sleeping, figuratively speaking. In hindsight, multiple signs were there for anyone to see. Because the military officers were not alert to the tell-tell signs, the attack was a complete and utter surprise. But even so, rarely is such an assault a total shock. The indicators for an attack were present but overlooked or not given proper weight that the situation demanded. This is a point to which believers in Jesus should pay attention so that we will not be caught off guard by a preemptive strike.

The D Day attack on June 6, 1944, was also an extreme surprise. The allied forces of the Americans, the Canadians, and the British besieged the German army on the beaches of Normandy, France. It was a bloody battle that stretched out over five beachheads. It was a hard fought battle, but ultimately declared a success. The attack was critical for ultimately bringing an end to World War II. The element of surprise was a major factor in the victory.

In what came to be known as the Six Day War, three armies prepared to attack Israel. On the morning of June 5, 1967, the Israeli army planned a preemptive strike against the Egyptian air force, destroying hundreds of planes that were on the ground. The Egyptians released a false report that they had defeated Israel. That false report prompted Jordan and Syria to join in the battle against Israel, whom they thought was crippled by a defeat from Egypt. On the ground, Israeli troops marched into the Sinai Peninsula and the Gaza Strip. They routed Palestinians from the West Bank of the Jordan River, seized the Golan Heights in Syria and continued on to the Suez Canal. The war ended with a cease fire in six days with Israel suffering only minimal losses compared to the catastrophic losses of their enemies. Israel tripled their territory in those six days. This amazing victory happened for two identifiable reasons. First, God fought for Israel (it has long been identified as a miraculous intervention) and second, Israel caught Egypt off guard.

Surprise in Spiritual Warfare

How does surprise apply in spiritual warfare? Surprise means to "attack or capture suddenly without warning" or to "cause astonishment or amazement." In the battle of the forces of God against the forces of darkness, believers often know a great deal about the enemy, but believers may be far too passive in overcoming him. How can believers surprise the enemy when we have to communicate in ways that could reveal our whole warfare strategy to the enemy in advance? How can believers plan without giving the enemy a long planning time to defeat, confuse, delay, or confound the plans of God's people? Our goals are to avoid being surprised but to bring surprise on our enemy!

Surprise is a great element of military strategy. Surprise creates a situation where victims are in shock, having been caught completely off guard. In the spiritual warfare of Christians against the kingdom of darkness, there are two facets of surprise: That of the believer and that of the enemy. First, there is no excuse for believers to ever be caught off guard. If believers are caught off guard, they have only to look to themselves because the information is there if people would care to seek it from the Lord. Prophets and others can know the plans of the Lord. The Holy Spirit recognizance about the plans of the enemy is available to believers. There must be systems in place to disseminate the information to the body of Christ for prayer and counter attack.

Second, believers may need to implement some strategies for catching the enemy off guard. The body of Christ in general does not appear to be very discreet or inconspicuous. In fact, the body of believers is often verbose about its activities, including strategic warfare. Surprise is an element of warfare that the body of Christ has not used effectively. Usually our tactics are telegraphed and discussed at great lengths before any event happens, giving the enemy time to plan a counter-offensive. How many times have great spiritual events been planned only to suffer delays, breakdowns, hindrances, attacks of many kinds? There are usually meetings upon meetings and discussions to plan. In fact, most Christians talk about

The Lord gave the strategy that it is safe to talk after worship, because the enemy will not remain in an extended period of worship. The enemy cannot stand to hear the praises of God and will flee from the heartfelt worship in Spirit and in truth.

everything that is important, but we do so at ill-advised times. We battle an invisible kingdom that is at work all around us. This alone is why praying in the spirit, known as praying in tongues, is critical for times of warfare. The spirit of a believer can communicate with the Father and the believer is built up, but the enemy is oblivious to the conversation. Praying in a prayer language facilitates surprise on the enemy.

I asked the question, "Lord, when is it safe to talk with other believers and not telegraph our plans to the enemy?" The Lord gave the strategy that it is safe to talk after worship because the enemy will not remain in an extended period of worship. The enemy cannot stand to hear the praises of God and will flee from the heartfelt worship of believers in spirit and in truth. I personally experienced demons fleeing during the times of worship.

When I was young in the faith, I had some interesting experiences month after month as I went to Emmaus gatherings. The Emmaus Walk was a seventy-two-hour retreat weekend of growth and spiritual renewal. After believers had been on one of the Emmaus Walks, they would gather for fellowship and worship once a month. The monthly meetings proved to be a gathering of Christian people who loved the Lord and wanted to serve him. The worship was always very sweet and heartfelt in a room of 200 to 300 hungry believers. At the time I was working as an attorney with my feet firmly planted in the world of courtroom drama and the intense and ugly arena of confrontation with other litigants. There were plenty of battleground skirmishes, emotional upheavals, anger, pride, jockeying for position and notice, among many other unholy thoughts and attitudes.

I noticed that every time I went to an Emmaus gathering, no matter how rested I was, I would first get sleepy and then I would start yawning. I would yawn my head off for several minutes during worship. I was fully engaged in the worship, and I was honoring God in those times with a heart to seek him. I noticed the strange phenomenon each month, but I could not account for the strange yawning occurrences. What I did not realize then, but later came to know, is that yawning was a form of deliverance. People who do a lot of deliverance ministry will confirm that demons leave through openings in the body: the mouth through coughs, yawns, or even vomit. They can depart in the form of tears, or even intestinal gas. As I had uncontrollable yawning during worship, it was actually the departure of demons that I had picked up, probably in my work since the previous month.

The best biblical example of demons leaving through bodily openings is found in 2 Kings. Elisha prayed for the Shunammite's son, and he was raised from the dead. The demons were released or expelled when the boy sneezed seven times. The story of the Shunammite's son being delivered from death is culminated in this way: "(Elisha) returned and walked back and forth in the house, and again went up and stretched himself out on him; *then the child sneezed seven times, and the child opened his eyes*" (2 Kings 4:35).

The bottom line is that demons depart during worship! I went to a conference with internationally known prophets. One of the conference speakers said, "Some demons will not depart without worship." They hang on through everything else, but when true and heartfelt worship occurs, they want to get away. This also reminds me of the discussion of the deaf and dumb spirit in an earlier chapter, about creating an atmosphere from which demons desire to flee. The demons do not have to be "cast out" but rather seek to escape from a holy atmosphere. Worship is a huge tool for deliverance and for changing the environment.

This gets back to the discussion of surprise. How can believers talk and maintain covert operations when there are invisible enemy spies around all the time? I originally asked the Lord when can believers safely talk without telling the enemy the strategic plans. The Lord answered, "When the atmosphere changes (after or during worship), it is safe to talk freely. If the atmosphere has not changed, it is not safe to talk without spies in the area." Of course, this rang true in my heart because of my experiences during the Emmaus monthly gatherings. The enemy cannot stand true worship, the blood of Jesus, praise, or praying in a prayer language because those things change the atmosphere and invite the presence of God.

When the presence of God is made known, demons want to flee. I have also seen this in Africa. When the presence of God showed up in a worship service, about forty people started having demonic manifestations at the same time. I learned at that time that demons show themselves, or depart if they are able, in the presence of the Spirit of God. They will do anything to avoid being in the presence of God. Discerning believers will know when the atmosphere has changed. People will know when God has come into the midst. That is when believers can talk and be strategic without the enemy knowing our plans.

One issue is that when the atmosphere changes, to indicate the presence of the glory of the Lord, no one wants to talk, they just want to enjoy the atmosphere of the presence of the Lord! However, during those times, the Lord does the talking and gives revelation, insight, discernment, words of knowledge, and brings confusion into the enemy's camp. During those times, the Spirit does the talking and people do not have to plan nearly as much as they thought they did. One problem is that when most believers have an agenda, they plan a meeting to form a plan. They usually plan no time on the schedule to worship or to create an atmosphere where the Lord is welcome and will lead the discussions. They just jump right into busyness.

Christians must never give information to the enemy. We must never take anything for granted. The devil is out to surprise us, so believers must not give him info that he needs to attack. Believers should take care to guard talk and keep it simple. It is also a matter of security. In the military, there is a saying, "Loose lips sink ships!" which is a warning to guard against loose talk that might be heard or intercepted by the wrong hands.

Tell all your needs to the Lord, and tell your victories to your friends. Speak and pray the answers, and not rehash the problems. Plan and strategize on critical warfare matters only after the atmosphere has been changed by worship of God. It is also a good policy to speak of your victories even if they have not manifested in the natural yet. They have been released in the heavenly realm. The enemy may be delaying them, but that does not change that the Lord has given us many gifts that are still waiting to manifest. Positive declaration is very important to seeing the full manifestation of God's kingdom on the earth as it is in heaven. Negative talk is the ammunition for the guns of the enemy to use against the troops in God's army. Hopelessness and doubt are fodder for the enemy's canons. Adequate security and intercession is what is needed to overcome surprise by the enemy against our team.

Passivity in the faith can also lead to surprise. Sometimes believers get surprised because it is invited by passivity. Refusal to take tactical measures leads to shock or astonishment. Believers do not have understanding of the element of surprise. Believers invite attacks by foolishness, passivity, prayerlessness, laziness, letting our guards down, busyness, or undisciplined behavior, to name a few. All of these things can lead to attack.

The devil is very clever to attack at just the right moment. He will hit hard. After the temptations of Jesus (and when Satan was not successful in derailing Jesus from God's plan), he pulled away from Jesus until a "more opportune time." If he was lurking around to see when Jesus was weak, we should expect nothing different. The enemy will try to deceive believers. Believers must not give the enemy any opportunity to use surprise against the body.

Deceive the enemy so that he reacts to the sight of his eyes. *The Art of War* is a classic military manual written by Sun Tzu in the 6th century B.C.[26] This manual is a mainstay for military strategy even in the current era. When showing how to catch the enemy unaware Sun Tzu said,

> All warfare is based on deception. Hence, when able to attack, we must seem unable; when using our forces, we must seem inactive; when we are near, we must make the enemy believe we are far away; when far away, we must make him believe we are near. ...If he is taking his ease, give him no rest. If his forces are united, separate them. Attack when he is unprepared, appear where you are not expected. These military devices, leading to victory, must not be divulged beforehand.[27]

The element of surprise also worked in the Bible. Many generals in God's army had surprise on their side, but they were not surprised. Surprise will work against the enemy but will never work against God's team members who are in strong relationship with the Lord. When God's team is listening, there is no surprise. Think how many times the enemy was defeated by surprise in the Word.

---

[26] Sun Tzu, *The Art of War*. Translated by Lionel Giles. The work is in the public domain.

[27] Ibid., part 1, paragraphs 18, 19, 23-25.

Remember an earlier chapter in which it was discussed that God is never surprised, therefore God's people should never be surprised.

Jehu was anointed to defeat and destroy the kingdom of Ahab and Jezebel. After he was anointed as king, he immediately set out to do the will of the Lord against Ahab and Jezebel's kingdom. He specifically told his compatriots not to let anyone talk about the things that he had shared with them about his anointing and call. He said, "If you are so minded, *let no one leave or escape from the city to go and tell it in Jezreel*" (2 Kings 9:15). He must have known the adage that, "Loose lips sink ships." He knew the importance of releasing information only at the right and proper time. With his commission to the men with him, he shut off the free flow of information to the enemy.

The story of Gideon is found in Judges 6 to 8. The Lord called him to lead the army against a far superior force. He culled the men down to 300 ready warriors. A careful reading of the Scripture illustrates that he did not tell the troops the full strategy until the battle was engaged. He told them they would know what to do by watching him. He was the only one who knew the full strategy:

> Then he divided the three hundred men into three companies, and he put a trumpet into every man's hand, with empty pitchers, and torches inside the pitchers. And he said to them, "*Look at me and do likewise; watch, and when I come to the edge of the camp you shall do as I do:* When I blow the trumpet, I and all who are with me, then you also blow the trumpets on every side of the whole camp, and say, "The sword of the Lord and of Gideon!" (Judg. 7:16-18)

Gideon did not tell them about breaking the vessels at the right time or holding up the torches. They only knew to do that by watching him:

> So Gideon and the hundred men who were with him came to the outpost of the camp at the beginning of

the middle watch, just as they had posted the watch; *and they blew the trumpets and broke the pitchers that were in their hands. Then the three companies blew the trumpets and broke the pitchers—they held the torches in their left hands and the trumpets in their right hands for blowing—and they cried,* "The sword of the LORD and of Gideon!" And every man stood in his place all around the camp; and the whole army ran and cried out and fled. (Judg. 7:19-21)

After the Midianite army was fully confused and started to retreat, then Gideon called the other forces to join in and help in the pursuit. The select warriors started the ball rolling with the surprise attack, but then the others joined in to finish off the enemy.

The Lord's people are not surprised when they listen. The enemy is not surprised when believers have loose lips. The enemy cannot hear the way God's people hear from the Lord. Satan is not all knowing; that is reserved for God alone. The enemy only has the strategy that he gets from observing and discerning. The enemy gains much info by listening and observing the people of God talk and see them act. Surprise is something that the Church has never learned to foster. It is a great tool. There are great lessons to be learned from Gideon: Take a few people and set a surprise ambush of the enemy camp. When the enemy is completely confused and routed, then the body of believers can join in and give pursuit.

Chapter 17

Pursuit

A leader who gives chase is a leader who will keep his victory. Pursuit is intentionally giving chase for the purpose to overtake, capture, or destroy. Field Marshall Viscount Allenby said during World War II, "While coolness in disaster is the supreme proof of a commander's courage, *energy in pursuit is the surest test of his strength of will*." In a warfare situation, pursuit of the enemy is hard. The reason that pursuit is a test of the will, as stated by Allenby, is that when a fighting force has had a victory and the enemy is retreating or fleeing, the temptation is to let up and enjoy the victory. The troops may be physically and mentally exhausted and can only think about resting after an intense battle. However, as Allenby stated, the strength of will, the will for ultimate and complete victory, is tested in pursuit. Complete victory is not achieved unless there is pursuit.

The Word of God gives evidence that pursuit is a strategy of the Lord. There are many warfare stories in the Old Testament that show pursuit after a battle. The book of Joshua also says, "One man of you shall *chase* a thousand, for the Lord your God is He who fights for you, as He promised you" (Josh. 23:10). Why do believers need strength of will to pursue? Because after a fierce battle, they are ready to let down. When victors in a battle let down short of complete domination of the enemy, they allow the enemy to regroup and mount up a resurgence against them. Resting in victory allows the enemy to come back.

There is another point to consider as well. A defeated army that is being chased will fight desperately because they are fighting for survival. They are fighting for life itself. Stated in spiritual terms, we know that Satan and his army are defeated. They are defeated, but they are fighting very hard to inflict every casualty that they possibly can. Not until the last enemy is defeated do believers deserve a rest. Our last enemy is death: "The last enemy that shall be destroyed is death" (1 Cor. 15:26). Believers are in a fierce battle until the end. Believers in Christ Jesus must pursue our enemy to overtake and destroy his plans and purposes.

It takes strength of will to enter into pursuit to utterly destroy the enemy. That is what will have to happen to defeat our foe. We cannot let the guard down one bit, or he will regroup and rise up again. Unless we pursue the demonic forces to destruction, the victory of the warfare cannot be preserved. Pursuit of the enemy can encompass such warfare tactics as prayer, fasting, worship of God, devotion, unity within the body of Christ, etc. These things weaken Satan and prevent his work from being allowed to continue. However, how many times has a great revival occurred, only to suffer setback or defeat because there is some sort of backlash by the demonic forces. Believers cannot let up to celebrate the victory, which only allows the enemy to regroup to come knocking again.

We are also in a battle against time to pursue the lost people of the world. We pursue the lost. One of our stated objectives is to make disciples of all nations. We make disciples out of converts. As long as we are on the planet, we do not give up, but rather keep pursuing. The Spirit of God will give the strength and the will of conviction to do so. In pursuit, believers must take care to maintain the pressure on the enemy until the victory is complete. Do not allow the enemy to escape. Annihilate the enemy.

In Judges 7, Gideon won a great victory in the Lord with three hundred men against a magnificent army. One might think that after a resounding victory that Gideon and the others would pause to catch their breaths to enjoy the miraculous and supernatural events of the day. After all, God had shown his mighty arm against a powerful foe. Who among us would not want to gather around the campfire to celebrate the miraculous occurrences and recount the greatness of God? I think that is our nature! Gideon did not react that way at all. He was thoroughly God's general, marshalling his troops to secure a great and decisive victory. What God started in the supernatural, Gideon finished in the natural. As we follow Gideon's story, we get a biblical perspective on pursuit. Judges 7 teaches a great deal about the manner and magnitude of pursuit.

> Then the three companies blew the trumpets and broke the pitchers—they held the torches in their left hands and the trumpets in their right hands for blowing—and they cried, "The sword of the Lord and of Gideon!" And every man stood in his place all around the camp; and *the whole army ran and cried out and fled*. When the three hundred blew the trumpets, *the Lord set* every man's sword against his companion throughout the whole camp; and *the army fled* to Beth Acacia, toward Zererah, as far as the border of Abel Meholah, by Tabbath. *And the men of Israel gathered together from Naphtali, Asher, and all Manasseh, and pursued the Midianites*. Then Gideon sent messengers throughout all the mountains of Ephraim, saying, "*Come down against the Midianites*, and seize from them the watering places as far as Beth Barah and the Jordan." Then all the men of Ephraim gathered together and seized the watering places as far as Beth Barah and the Jordan. And they captured two princes of the Midianites, Oreb and Zeeb. They killed Oreb at the rock of Oreb, and Zeeb they killed at the winepress of Zeeb. *They pursued Midian and brought the heads of Oreb and Zeeb to Gideon on the other side of the Jordan*. (Judg. 7:15-25)

There can be no doubt that God gave Gideon the victory. Recall that Gideon culled his army from 32,000 to 300. Some were in fear;

he sent them home. Some were culled in other ways. Gideon's army was far outnumbered *before they were culled*. After the excess of the army was removed, it would have been ludicrous to take on the battle, ... but for the hand of God in the situation. God did what he promised he would do and that was give Gideon a great victory. The victory was already in the bag, but Gideon gave chase anyway.

There are some other warfare points to note. The company of men, the 300 men who were left, were well organized. Gideon was leading by example and cooperation. He was a leader/general who was close to the action. Gideon was in complete control of every person on the battlefield. They had to watch him to know what to do. They had to act all together in unity. He did not give them the complete plan; they had to watch him to know how and when to act. He was in complete control of the troops. An apostolic leader should never lose control of that which the Lord has put into his or her hand. A great leader is in charge. They get control and keep control. That is what apostles do.

Gideon had the warfare elements of surprise, concentration, economy of force, mobility, and offensive. The Midianite army was instantly on the defensive. There was no cooperation in the enemy force. There was no unity of the enemy's camp. The Midianites did not stay cool in the face of disaster. They retreated in complete chaos. The enemy lost complete control of the situation. If the Midianite army had been adequately commanded, they would have had plans and contingency plans. They would have known how to react in the situation. Apparently, there was no plan laid down about how to handle the contingency of surprise.

The main point is that after the initial battle and retreat of the opposing army, as they were fleeing the field of battle, Gideon pursued and called others to pursue with him. He had the enemy on the run,

It is a mistake, upon achieving an apparent victory over low level demons, to think that the battle has been won. In warfare when the leaders are intact, the troops have someone to follow. With leadership, the troops can be reformed into a fighting contingency again.

and he did not let up until the opposition was completely decapi-tated. Not only did he pursue, he called in reinforcements to pursue with him. He did not even stop when the heads of the princes of Midian were presented to him. But that is not all. Look even beyond to what happened in the next chapter of the book of Judges: "When Gideon came to the Jordan, he and the three hundred men who were with him crossed over, *exhausted but still in pursuit*" (Judg. 8:4). They were not going to give up, no matter how weary and spent they were. They were going after the generals of the army. They were not satisfied with the decapitation of the princes of Midian, the lower level leaders. They needed to capture and kill the kings of Midian, so that the army would have no leaders to rally behind again. This is a lesson for believers: We must not give up on the pursuit until the ultimate leaders are completely debilitated.

This is a picture of what happens in spiritual warfare. As I have seen in deliverance ministry, often the high level demons will send out the low level demons first. It is a mistake, upon achieving an apparent victory over low level demons, to think that the battle has been won. The high ranking demons hope that believers will think that they have won the ultimate victory, not give pursuit, and go home to enjoy the victory. If the high level demons in charge of the situation are not dealt with, they just regroup and regain strength and come back for another round of attack. In warfare, when the leaders are intact, the troops have someone to follow. With leadership, the troops can be reformed into a fighting contin-gency again. However, when the leaders are eliminated, the troops will not reform to mount a counter offensive: "Strike the Shepherd, and the sheep will be scattered" (Zech. 13:7).

Look further to what happened in the Gideon story as he pur-sued the kings of Midian: "When Zebah and Zalmunna fled, *he pursued them;* and *he took the two kings of Midian, Zebah and Zalmunna, and routed the whole army*" (Judg. 8:12). When the kings were captured the whole army scattered. When the two kings were captured, the army was thoroughly defeated. Gideon main-tained pressure of the offensive in pursuit until he had obtained the objective. To see Gideon's objective, look at what the Lord said during Gideon's original call before the battle ensued:

"The Lord is with you, you mighty man of valor!"
… Then the Lord turned to him and said, "Go in
this might of yours, and you shall save Israel from
the hand of the Midianites. Have I not sent you?"…
And the Lord said to him, "*Surely I will be with you,
and you shall defeat the Midianites as one man.*"
(Judg. 6:12,14,16)

Gideon's call and purpose was to lead Israel to defeat the
Midianites as one man. Gideon was not to do it alone, but Israel
needed a general to rally behind. God will call those generals who
will rally the troops. Gideon was not called to watch them flee.
He was called to decimate them. His objective was to thoroughly
defeat them, and he fulfilled his objective.

In the war with those in the camp of Satan, believers can learn
from some of the warfare tactics of the great generals of the earth
and of the Bible. Listening to the Holy Spirit for strategy of knowledge is the most effective tool for utter defeat of the enemy. Follow
up prayer is very important, as well as instruction in the Word of the
Lord. The Word reminds us time and again that we are to engage
in warfare. Our objective is set forth in the Word or by strategies
released by the Holy Spirit. We are to fulfill our objective and
pursue the enemy to utter defeat! The book of Job talks about the
pursuit of the wicked, "He is driven from light into darkness, and
chased out of the world" (Job 18:18). God intends for the wicked to
be chased and pursued and defeated. It is our calling and the stated
objective of the body of Christ under firm and anointed apostolic
leadership. The book of Isaiah says, "The nations shall rush like
the rushing of many waters: but God shall rebuke them, and they
*shall flee far off, and shall be chased as the chaff of the mountains
before the wind*, and like a rolling thing before the whirlwind" (Isa.
17:13). Believers give chase; it honors the Lord.

Chapter 18

Mobility

I was talking to a prayer partner and she said, "I need to make some confessions. I am bogged down in the spirit. I cannot get up and get motivated to do what I need to do. I am having trouble knowing what to read in the Word. I am just bogged down." She was suffering from hindrance of her mobility in the realm of God's kingdom. To be bogged down means to become encumbered and slow. It is as if one is walking through a bog or in deep mud, which is drudgery and results in trudging. The legs become weighted down and heavy. When bogged down, a person is prevented from making progress. It is toil and grinding. It is lumbering awkwardly along burdened by cares and even invisible hindrances. Those who are bogged down are not mobile in the spirit realm or in the natural realm.

If an army is bogged down, it may miss the opportunity presented at that moment to secure a strategic position or even a victory. An army that is bogged down is not mobile and that is dangerous because it takes away the ability to be on the offensive. In fact, an army that is bogged down is like a sitting duck. On the other hand, if we see a weakness of the enemy's camp, we can fill the gap and bog the enemy down. The goal, like so many in this book, is not to be bogged down, but work in the kingdom realm to bog the enemy down so that the enemy forces are ineffective in all they attempt to do.

It is important for believers in God's army not to be bogged down with non-essentials. Often people to get weighted down and overlook the things of God for the cares of the moment. In the parable of the soils, the third soil represents the state of being bogged down. The Lord said, "And some (seed) fell among thorns, and the thorns sprang up and choked them" (Matt. 13:7). When he explained the parable, he said: "Now he who received seed among the thorns is *he who hears the word, and the cares of this world and the deceitfulness of riches choke the word, and he becomes unfruitful*" (Matt. 13:22). In this parable, the person heard the Word, but cares and deceit choked out the Word. Being bogged down ultimately means to become unfruitful. Unfruitful vines are ultimately cast into the fire. It is critical not to remain unfruitful even if we become bogged down for a moment.

The first step to overcome a lack of mobility in the spirit is to recognize that we are bogged down. Fasting, prayer, and daily reading in God's word are strategies that will help a person overcome a bogged state. Sometimes a person must simply choose to exercise self-will to get up and get back in the battle or to rekindle the relationship with the Lord. Being bogged down simply means that the enemy has put some weights on the spiritual legs. It is as if an old-time prisoner's ball and chain is attached to the leg that must be severed. The enemy wants to keep believers slow of foot and unable to be fleet to carry out the will and wishes of the Lord.

A spiritual mentor told me a truth that is worthy to be repeated here: "The more you advance in Christian service, the fewer choices that you have." He had to explain that the higher the calling, the narrower the calling. The narrower the calling, the fewer opportunities there are for extras in life. The more the Lord is Master of a life, the less time there is for fluff. Pruning is required. The higher a believer goes, the more he or she will have to constantly sensor activities of life.

I have seen that in my own life. The more I have served the Lord and dedicated my life to him, the less time and opportunity I have had for extracurricular activities. They may not be bad things, but they are not God things either. I rarely watch TV, go to the movies; my life is pretty much given over to the Lord. A few years ago, when I was just starting this journey with the Lord, I received a prophetic word. I did not even know what a prophetic word was, and it was the first one I ever received that I remember. The lady stood and pointed to me in a crowd (I looked over my shoulder to see who she was talking to...). She said, "Do not let the good things get in the way of the God things." I have carried that word with me for almost ten years as of the writing of this book. I have never forgotten that, and that word has shaped my actions many times as I sought to discern if something was merely a "good thing" or a "God thing." Good things, while not inherently bad, will steal time from the things that God has for us to do. It is a matter of dedication and the level of heart devotion to the Lord. Will we be whole-hearted, half-hearted, or cold-hearted?

It is important for believers, and in fact, the body of Christ as a whole, to be very mobile so that we can be ready to go at a moment's notice. The opposite of being bogged down is being mobile. In the story of Phillip and the Ethiopian eunuch, Phillip left in a minute's notice and went where the Lord told him to go. Acts 8 says, "Now an angel of the Lord spoke to Philip, saying, "'Arise and go toward the south along the road which goes down from Jerusalem to Gaza.' This is desert. *So he arose and went*" (Acts 8:26-27a). Later, after Phillip ministered to the Ethiopian eunuch, he was caught away by the Spirit of God:

> So (the eunuch) commanded the chariot to stand still. And both Philip and the eunuch went down into the water, and he baptized him. Now when they came up out of the water, the Spirit of the Lord caught Philip away, so that the eunuch saw him no more; and he went on his way rejoicing. *But Philip was found at Azotus. And passing through, he preached in all the cities till he came to Caesarea.* (Acts 8:38-40)

Look what happened to Phillip in Acts 8 after he ministered and baptized the man. He was caught away to Azotus and preached in all the cities until he came to Caesarea. He went out for a short trek to the south road and ended up on an extended missionary journey. People who are not mobile cannot do that. People who are bogged down with life's cares and possessions will not be able to leave instantly at the call of God. Only people who have their affairs in order can leave on such short notice and be at the will and impulse of the Holy Spirit.

In getting bogged down, often the first things to go are prayer or communion with God and Bible reading. When the basics of maintaining a relationship with God fall away, it is then that believers can quickly become bogged down with secondary matters.

Another thing that comes under attack from the enemy is the senseless demands on time. Believers must maintain mobility with time. Once time is gone, it is gone forever. God is outside of time. He is not limited by time as human beings are. However, in our frail human condition, time is fleeting and once it is stolen or squandered, there is no redeeming it without the intervention of the Lord. Paul cautioned believers: *"See then that you walk circumspectly, not as fools but as wise*, redeeming the time, because the days are evil" (Eph. 5:15-16). There must be ruthless attention to the things that steal time. Believers should endeavor to eliminate anything that gets in the way of achieving the objectives of God! People who squander time are fools according to the words of Paul in Ephesians 5.

Another caution is to protect the spirit, soul, and body! Paul calls for sanctification, to be set apart for God's use and service, so that all of the being of a human is preserved. Paul writes, "Now may the God of peace Himself sanctify you completely; and may your whole spirit, soul, and body be preserved blameless at the coming of our Lord Jesus Christ" (1 Thes. 5:23).

A huge factor in mobility is the maintenance of the body. Believers must care for the body. Take care of the body with careful and daily maintenance. Care for the body, but do not pamper it. It is the body that

"God gave me a message to deliver and a horse to ride. Alas, I have killed the horse and cannot deliver the message." Believers are the horse with the message; do not kill the horse.

will carry a believer to the place of usefulness to the Lord. If the body does not function, the call of a person may be severely limited by the lack of mobility.

Robert Murray M'Cheyne was one of the most powerful ministers to ever stand in the pulpits of Scotland. He died at the age of twenty-nine, partly because he worked so hard that his health broke. He suffered from excessive busyness and chronic fatigue. Some of his dying words were, "God gave me a message to deliver and a horse to ride. Alas, I have killed the horse and cannot deliver the message."[28] The apostle Paul said to the church at Ephesus, "Therefore take heed to yourselves and to all the flock, among which the Holy spirit has made you overseers" (Acts 20:28). If we do not take care of ourselves, we cannot take care of whatever flock God has given us.

Most great men and women of the faith could probably be called extremist because they are or have been radical activists of the faith. However, believers have to maintain balance even amidst extremism for God! Peter Marshall was a former Chaplin of the U.S. Senate. A friend asked him after a heart attack, "I am curious to know something. What did you learn during your illness?" He replied, "I learned that the Kingdom of God goes on without Peter Marshall."[29] Indeed, this is a good lesson for every believer who is tempted to think that they are something so special that the world will not spin without them pushing the peddles to make it go. Overinflated egos have been the bane and downfall of many good soldiers for Christ.

Do not take anything that is not absolutely necessary into battle; maintain mobility in all areas of life. That means not only physical needs but also, maintain health and purity in the soul and in the spirit, as well. Missionary William Burns was a missionary to China. After he died abroad, his few meager possessions were sent home to his friends. The small box of possessions was opened by a group who had gathered around. They discovered a few items including a few sheets of paper with notes, a Chinese Bible, an English Bible, a writing case, one Chinese dress, a couple of books,

---

[28] https://bible.org/illustration/killed-horse. Accessed June 28, 2017.
[29] https://bible.org/illustration/killed-horse. Accessed June 28, 2017.

and a Chinese lantern.[30] One of the children present said, "Surely, surely he must have been very poor." Joseph Carroll said, "He was not poor, but very rich. He was a good soldier, stripped to the bone and he was mobile!"[31]

In this book, we have addressed the issue of surprise for military supremacy. Surprise also depends on being able to move forces fast and hit the enemy before they know what hit them. Surprise and mobility depend on not getting bogged down with unessential activities or possessions. In mobility, each person must be willing to deprive him or herself of the small personal plan for the sake of the master plan. This is a truth to which countless persecuted and martyred Christians can attest.

---

[30] https://books.google.com/books?id=VVwEAAAAQAAJ&pg=PA63&d-q=william+burns+missionary+to+china+possessions&hl=en&sa=X-&ved=0ahUKEwj854yqmubUAhWIKiYKHeHSDxMQ6AEIQzAF-#v=onepage&q=william%20burns%20missionary%20to%20china%20possessions&f=false. Accessed June 27, 2017.

[31] See previous Footnote about Joseph Carroll.

Chapter 19

Economy of Force

Economy of force is the principle of employing all available combat power in the most effective way possible. It is an attempt to use the minimum essential combat power in any secondary effort so that the main fighting force is directed toward the ultimate objective of the war. It is the prudent use of military forces towards the primary objective in any conflict. The goals are that no part of a force should ever be left without a clearly defined purpose and that no part of a force is worn out by overwork where the force is not needed.

Every person in the body of Christ has a divine purpose and that purpose must be employed for the body to function well as a massive military organization. The problem occurs when soldiers in God's army do not know their gift or calling. There is a discussion of the purpose of individuals in the companion book, *Leader!* One function of apostolic leaders is to help people find their purpose and to get into their call. There can never be total economy of force in God's army as long as people are not fulfilling their call and purpose. When each individual in God's army of believers fully understands his or her purpose and fulfills that God-given purpose, the body of Christ will function like a well-oiled machine.

Carl von Clausewitz said that "Every unnecessary expenditure of time, every unnecessary detour, is a waste of power, and therefore contrary to the principles of strategy."[32] Efficiency is the key to using forces wisely. Some people can accomplish with three people what others cannot accomplish with ten. The difference is efficiency in use of the resources.

Gideon culled his army to 300 brave soldiers. When Gideon sent 31,700 men home to win with 300 soldiers, he was using the minimum force possible to defeat the opposing army. Twenty-two thousand men were afraid to go into battle. Ninety-seven hundred were not ready to go, so they were dismissed. They were culled by the standard set by God (Judg. 7). Gideon made the right decision to dismiss the ones who were fearful, unprepared, and unready to war in the conflict. Prudence says, "Let them go; they are not good soldiers anyway." It proved to be better to go into battle with a handful of soldiers who were mentally, spiritually, and physically ready than with a massive army of ill-equipped soldiers.

Only a fraction qualified for a position in Gideon's army. Gideon trained a handful who could do the job. This small fighting force was used in the right place at the right time by the leading of the Lord. When Gideon went into battle position, he achieved surprise that led to a great victory against a superior enemy. He could never have surprised the enemy with 32,000 men. Only because of the limitation of the fighting contingency, was Gideon able to achieve the level of surprise that he did. The clearly defined objective was to defeat Midian. When they were on the run, he called all the remaining soldiers to join in the pursuit.

As the leadership in the body of believers implements this principle, there will be culling of the force. There will be some who are afraid to fight the enemy, and they will take themselves out of the battle. There will be some who are culled for other reasons. Some may have open sin, and they cannot get in the battle or they will be wounded or worse. There are some who are simply lazy, asleep, unconcerned, or dull in the spirit. Those people will be culled because they do not have a heart for the things of God and they do not love the things that God loves.

Economy of force only works when the objective is fully known. If there is uncertainty or confusion about the objective,

---

[32] Clausewitz's On War, J. J. Graham translation published in London in 1873.

there will be no economy of force because the temptation will be to throw all available resources toward an offensive. In other words, when the plan is broad and general, such as to "defeat the enemy," the feeling is that everyone just needs to "do something" to achieve that objective. However, if there is a clearly defined objective, such as to bring a transformation in local government, the objective may be met by having godly people run for office and by having regular pinpointed intercessory prayer. The objectives are concise and stated so that a handful of people could implement a plan to fulfill those concise and well-defined objectives. Where there is a general objective, or no objective at all, there is no good plan in place to effectuate change. The energy and forces are more easily scattered if there is no clear objective. In that circumstance, leaders cannot concentrate forces on the clearly defined objective because it does not exist.

Being able to have a clearly defined objective comes from concentration on what God wants believers to do. When we do only what the Lord says, the objective and the strategy will be well known. As with Gideon, the Lord will establish what human resources are needed to do the job and to give God all the glory. Believers should never participate in anything that God is not calling forth. It comes down to one of three things: Being out of God's will, being in God's permissive will, or being in God's sovereign perfect will. Romans 12:2 shows that there are levels of God's will for humanity: "And do not be conformed to this world, but be transformed by the renewing of your mind, that you may prove what is that *good and acceptable and perfect* will of God."

During my lifetime, I have observed that there are some things that are absolutely against God's will. There are some things that are permissive, which would be acceptable either way. There are some things that are God's sovereign will. If a person refuses to do them, that person is in disobedience. Once my husband and I were planning a mission trip to Africa. About one month before the trip, the Lord pulled the plug on my attendance. He simply and clearly said, "You will not go!" I knew that for me to go was against the absolute will of God in that situation. To go would have been utter disobedience. I pulled off the team even though I was the ministry team leader, had been leading training sessions for weeks, and already had my airline ticket.

My husband wondered if he should go without me. I prayed and heard, "He *can* go." It was not, "He must go," or "He must not go." It was a permissive thing as if God said, "He can go if he wants to." Permissive will is not God's best, but it is not really disobedience to do it either. It was disobedience for me to go; it was permissive for him to go. I stayed home, but he went. He did not have the protection of being in the perfect will of God. I had the protection of being in the perfect will of God by staying home. On the trip, my husband contracted malaria while he was there and nearly died, spending six days in the hospital. That taught us something about doing things in the permissive will of God. We have a policy that if it is not God's sovereign will or perfect will, we will hardly do it. Permissive will causes dilution of forces. People may not be in their gift or calling, so they may not be doing what God needs them to do at that moment. To use economy of force, the troops must be prepared for the task at hand, being prepared in every way.

Joshua was sent by God into the Promised Land, to route all the enemies of God's people and take the land for Israel. Joshua had one victory under his belt in taking the city of Jericho. He sent a relatively small fighting force to capture the next city, Ai. Joshua was trying to conserve his force when he sent troops into battle for Ai. Conquering Ai was his primary objective, but he did not treat it as such in Joshua 7:

> Now Joshua sent men from Jericho to Ai, which is beside Beth Aven, on the east side of Bethel, and spoke to them, saying, "Go up and spy out the country." So the men went up and spied out Ai. And they returned to Joshua and said to him, "*Do not let all the people go up, but let about two or three thousand men go up and attack Ai. Do not weary all the people there, for the people of Ai are few.*" So about three thousand men went up there from the people, but they fled before the men of Ai. (Josh. 7:2-4)

Joshua was not prudent when he sent what he thought should have been an ample force to capture Ai. He was trying to economize his forces and not wear out all the people. His primary objective was to have conquest and settlement of the Promised Land. His

John Wesley said, "Give me one hundred men who fear nothing but sin and desire nothing but God, and I care not whether they be clergyman or laymen, they alone will shake the gates of Hell and set up the kingdom of Heaven upon the earth."

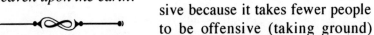

plan to conserve his troops backfired when he had an open door to sin in the camp. Joshua was surprised and defeated by an inferior force because there was sin in the camp when one man brought in polluted items. Also, God did not tell him to economize his troops; he would have been better off if he had sent in the whole army.

Believers can be on the offensive because it takes fewer people to be offensive (taking ground) than it does to be defensive (guarding against an attack). The person attacking has the advantage of knowing the point at which he can attack and where the attack will be. Maintaining the offensive makes the best use of forces. In spiritual warfare, believers often do not need a huge force to obtain a victory. John Wesley said, "Give me one hundred men who fear nothing but sin and desire nothing but God, and I care not whether they be clergyman or laymen, they alone will shake the gates of Hell and set up the kingdom of Heaven upon the earth."[33]

There is a huge battle in the heavenly realm. In a recent battle that I was in, the strategic leader who was leading the charge said, "I do not want quantity, I want quality of forces." He would rather have a few highly trained and battle ready intercessors with an anointing for the job, than a large force who was not ready. Economy of force also includes the necessity of having well-trained soldiers. Believers do not have to let people know that they are on the offensive, but the plan is to not give the enemy any rest. The fewer who know the plans and strategies, the fewer people there

---

[33] https://blog.logos.com/2011/04/ten_thought-provoking_john_wesley_quotes. Accessed June 26, 2017.

are to convey the plans to the enemy. Security is important. If the enemy does not know the plans, he cannot meet the attack. If he knows the offensive maneuver before it is made, he will meet the attack with a much greater oppositional force.

Economy of force allows for concentration of forces where they are needed, but where there is no waste. Over-concentration of forces where they are not needed is a waste of resources. Believers should be careful that they give their time where it best serves the Lord. If not careful, believers can concentrate energies on things that do not really matter to the Lord, or are not productive for advancing his kingdom. If that is the case, they may never have a decisive victory in any place or at any time.

Chapter 20

Focus On Focus

The Lord said to me, "Focus on your focus." That could mean to have a clear and sharp image of that which is the center point of the attention. Focus is about knowing what is the center of one's attention and bringing it into sharp clarity and understanding. The focus should always be the Lord and not the enemy. The point of any believer's attention and attraction and activity is the Lord, and none other. When a believer begins to put too much attention on the enemy, the clarity of the image gets blurred. The main attention should always be on the Lord.

Focus is critical for the body of believers. Focus requires concentration. Focus brings things to mind that are there, but would not be seen if a person did not stop to pause and intentionally notice. Being alert has saved many saints from destruction and lack of focus has cost many believers his or her life. Being in focus has allowed many people to grow into a deeper relationship with the Lord. Focus will allow room, or margin, for the Holy Spirit to speak. On the other hand, if a believer floats along, not thinking about the Lord, that person may miss opportunities to receive very important words or deepen his or her relationship with God.

Focus is not the same thing as being *in focus* or being *out of focus*.

- *Focus* is the point of attention or activity.
- *Being in focus* is to have a clear and sharp image.

178

- *To focus* is to bring adjustments to a lens to produce a clear image.
- *Being out of focus* is to have a blurry image that eliminates the details from perception.

Probably one of the most common points of reference of focus is that of a camera lens. A camera that is out of focus is not worth much because it cannot perform the function for which it was intended, which is to take clear and perfect pictures. A picture out of focus muddles the details. A common statement is that, "The devil is in the details." The things that are missed when things are out of focus are the fine details that can make the difference between winning and losing. When the view of a believer is out of focus and the devil is in the details, the believer is caught unaware of the hazards that are right before him. Focus brings things in the lens into clear view. The details are crisp and clear and readily apparent to the eye.

We glance at the enemy, but we gaze on our Lord! The point is that the Lord deserves our loving gaze and devotion. We must never give the enemy the glory that belongs to the Lord by giving more attention to him and his activities than to the Lord.

Out of Focus

I always like to say, "We glance at the enemy, but we gaze on our Lord!" I have said that so long that I am not sure if I heard it or if I made it up. The point is that the Lord deserves our gaze and devotion. We must never give the enemy the glory that belongs to the Lord by giving more attention to him and his activities than to the Lord. As the Lord is the center of the attention, as we focus in on the Lord, the things that have been blurry and out of focus become clear.

Even some can have the Lord as the main focus, but even so, the view of him is distorted and out of focus. The prayer to be prayed is that the object of our attention comes into clear focus for everyone in the body of believers. This distortion occurs when error comes in and people do not know that they are in error: "Be diligent to present yourself approved to God, a worker who does not need to be ashamed, *rightly dividing the word of truth*" (2 Tim. 2:15). If Paul cautioned Timothy to rightly divide the Word of truth, that means that it can be wrongly divided! There are times when even believers wander from the truth. They must be turned back so that they can be saved: "Brethren, *if anyone among you wanders from the truth*, and someone turns him back, let him know that he who turns a sinner from the error of his way will save a soul from death and cover a multitude of sins" (James 5:19-20). Paul cautioned Timothy to be focused and alert because in the evil days ahead, the people will turn their ears from sound doctrine. They will lose the focus on the Lord and be drawn away to other things:

> Preach the word! Be ready in season and out of season. Convince, rebuke, exhort, with all longsuf-fering and teaching. For the time will come when they will not endure sound doctrine, but according to their own desires, because they have itching ears, they will heap up for themselves teachers; and *they will turn their ears away from the truth*, and be turned aside to fables. (2 Tim. 4:2-4)

When believers are out of clarity, it is necessary to bring adjust-ments to bring things into clear view. The problem comes when people are in error and they have trouble discerning the Word of truth from the error. In the days ahead, if it is not already, the spirit of error will be a huge problem for the body of believers. The people who do not keep their focus sharp with the Lord as the center of their attention will lose the right and proper focus:

> *Beloved, do not believe every spirit, but test the spirits*, whether they are of God; because many false prophets have gone out into the world. By this you know the Spirit of God: Every spirit that confesses that Jesus Christ has come in the flesh is of God, and every spirit that does not confess that Jesus Christ has come in the flesh is not of God. And this

is the spirit of the Antichrist, which you have heard
was coming, and is now already in the world. *You
are of God, little children, and have overcome them,
because He who is in you is greater than he who
is in the world.* They are of the world. Therefore,
they speak as of the world, and the world hears
them. We are of God. He who knows God hears
us; he who is not of God does not hear us. *By this
we know the spirit of truth and the spirit of error.*
(1 John 4:1-3,6)

People bring things into clarity in the Word, in fellowship, in
listening, and meditation on Scriptures or godly counsel. That is
what happens when people begin to focus. Focus leads to the right
and proper attention and keeps believers from losing relationship
with the Spirit of Truth, and being drawn away to the spirit of error.

Having Your Focus in Focus

The Lord showed me the library of heaven in a vision. I came
away from that experience knowing that the knowledge of God is
beyond human understanding, but God's knowledge is available to
those who seek to find it. It is not merely knowledge for knowledge
sake, but rather it is about pursuing God and knowing Him! The
Lord illustrated it to me in terms I could understand. The Lord's
knowledge covers everything, but yet people have not understood.
They do not see the truth. It is with them always, but it is like things
before the time of revelation. It is there. It is like reading a Scripture
many times with no special revelation before its time. Then one
day, something special, that has been there all the time, is revealed
and the spiritual eyes are opened.

Knowledge is the key. I have been praying for it for a long time.
The Lord hears the prayers of his people for revelation. Some have
already been seeking; some will begin the quest now. Pray that the
Lord puts the desire in each one to have more knowledge, understanding, discernment, and revelation. Seek after him and he will
show the hungry ones great and unsearchable things that they (nor
anyone else) yet knows.

The Lord said to me, "Pursuit is a visible image of a deepening relationship." When my husband was first interested in dating me, he asked me out, but I was dating another young man. I even fixed him up on a blind date. I ran into him a few times, but I was still attached in a dating relationship. A few months later, I ran into him at a Disco. Yes, it was the early 1980s! When he found out that I was unattached, he asked to take me home, but I had driven my car. He was persistent for many months before we finally went out on a date. He pursued me. We both know now that the relationship between us was ordained by God, but that was far from our minds at the time. He was following the lead of the Holy Spirit even then.

The Lord spoke to me about that one day and said, "Your husband pursued you at first when you were starting to know each other. Then the relationship got comfortable and at peace. You both knew that you had each other, and that neither one of you is going anywhere or in search of any other relationship."

The Spirit of God spoke in terms of my relationship with the Lord, "In the pursuit, there is a revelation that there is interest. In your pursuit of me, I know that you want more of me, and it is a blessing to me. In Mike's pursuit of you, you knew that he was interested in you. He was a man who knew what he wanted and he went after it. As you pursue me, it opens up a place for more knowledge and more intimacy in the relationship."

This idea of focus really comes down to a deepening relationship with the Lord. As people seek to put him in the center of their attention, they begin pursuit. Just as my husband was a man who knew what he wanted in a relationship with me, I know that I am hungry for a deepening relationship with the Lord. My prayer is this: "Lord I am hungry for more of you. I do not know what to do to deepen the relationship except to go after you with everything I have in me, leaving all behind. Lord I am ready to leave everything behind. I am ready to turn back to you and be fully yours." This is a prayer of pursuit. If it speaks to you, make it your prayer or pray one from your own heart. Pursue him and make him the center of your focus.

Even though life gets in the way at times, it is right to focus on the Lord and the love of the Lord. The Lord has seen the needs of his people and he knows the pain and heartache of his precious ones. He feels pain more intently and intimately than people feel their own pain. People who are in a human body and with human senses are dulled compared to those in the Spirit. Humanity lives in a world that is replete with dullness. There are times that people have struggled not to be dull. It is a fact of the human condition without the knowledge of God: "Everyone is dull-hearted, without knowledge" (Jer. 51:17).

Can people change their human condition of dullness? Can people be more spiritually alive and more focused on the things of the Spirit and have more discernment? The answer is, "Yes!" A person has to be willing to be more spiritually aware of what is going on around them in an invisible realm. Once that change is brought forth, and the eyes of the spirit are opened and brought into clarity in the spiritual realm, it will not be undone. So the question must be asked, "Lord, can I stand the change to greater spiritual awareness? Lord, have others stood it before?" Yes, many in fact, but it can bring great joy and great sorrow. What happens is that people begin to see things in the light of the realm of the Spirit. It can be intense.

Every person must ask, "Lord, do you think that I am ready for that?" How do people prepare for a greater and more intense relationship with the Lord where the dullness of the human condition is removed? This reminds me of many near death experiences where people experience the heavenly realm or even the realm of the kingdom of darkness. In the underworld there is no light, and the darkness is smothering and intensely frightful. In the heavenly realm, the colors are so vibrant and alive that people do not have an adequate vocabulary to describe what they have seen. Humanity on earth is caught in the middle of the spectrum, not blinded by the darkness, but not fully able to experience the intensity of the heavenly realm.

The preparation for experiencing more of God's kingdom on the earth is a matter of the heart. It is born out of a desire of the heart to know the Lord more intimately. Even when a person has that desire, distractions must be eliminated. Often eliminating the distractions is a force of total will of the person to seek God and not let the world crowd out the desire to seek God.

It is a matter of focusing one's focus! Cultivate focus for a few minutes at a time. Set a timer for one minute and think of nothing but God. Allow the mind to go only where the Holy Spirit goes. Then increase the time to two minutes and continue to lengthen out the time focusing on the Lord. In the process of sitting before the Lord with intensity in focus, something will begin to happen. The Lord will begin to open up the heavenly realm to greater understanding. Relationship is a thing of this age. In heaven there will be no "relationship" because believers will all be abiding in his presence. Knowledge is the same way. In the end, love will win. There will not be "knowledge" because all will be known: "For now, we see in a mirror, dimly, but then face to face. *Now I know in part, but then I shall know just as I also am known*" (1 Cor. 13:12). When in heaven together, there will be no need of revealed knowledge; all will be revealed. On earth revelation is in part. In the heavenly realm, there is full knowing and full intimacy. Abiding is about knowing and being known. As people abide in the Lord and his Word, and him in his people, they come to know him more. I continue to pray, "Lord, please tell me what I need to do to grow the relationship on earth."

I implored, "Lord, please teach me. Please, please teach me your promises of Jeremiah 33:3. Lord, you are unsearchable. That means I cannot find the unsearchable things without you revealing them to me. God, please tell me. God, I am calling to you in faith and in humility, knowing that I am not worthy and have no special place other than I am standing on your promises and I am hungry! Please, God!"

The Lord said, "Laura, the greater good is the key to all blessings and knowledge." He showed me these words: *"But the manifestation of the Spirit is given to each one for the profit of all"* (1 Cor. 12:7). As believers seek to use what he reveals for the greater good of his people and his kingdom, more will be revealed by the Lord.

A Message from the Author

Laura Henry Harris

I was an attorney for twenty years before leaving the practice of law to be in full time service to the Lord. That service has looked like many different things in the last several years. I attended Asbury Theological Seminary and United Theological Seminary, obtaining a Masters of Divinity and a Doctor of Ministry degree. I served as a pastor of a United Methodist Church for four years. I have traveled to many countries around the world for missions and ministry. Perhaps the greatest joy of my service to the Lord is to seek to hear his voice and to teach revelation of Scripture that the Lord has revealed to me. I am always interested in opportunities to teach and equip the body of believers, especially ministry leaders.

I intersect with believers from around the world through written works and social media, as well as travel. Our ministry is called "Where He Leads Me, Inc." Free teaching videos are available on the Web address. Other books are available on the web page or at on-line sources in either print or electronic forms. Check out Amazon, Kindle, iBook, and Nook.

Postal address:
Dr. Laura Henry Harris
P.O. Box 459
Columbia, KY 42728

Email:
WhereHeLeadsMeInfo@gmail.com

Webpage:
whereheleadsme.org

Facebook:
Where He Leads Me, Inc.

OTHER WORKS BY LAURA HENRY HARRIS

Leader!
An End Time Guide for Apostolic Leaders

L *eader!* was birthed on the isle of Patmos, where John received the book of Revelation. The author Laura Harris went to Patmos specifically to seek the Lord. Immediately, the Lord began to teach her about preparation of apostolic leaders for what will be required in the days ahead. *Leader!* is designed to help apostles and other forerunners equip themselves and the Church to bring godly order.

If the body of Christ cannot handle the challenges of the peaceful times, how will it handle the challenges of the hard times. The Lord questioned Jeremiah saying, "If you have run with the footmen, and they have wearied you, then how can you contend with horses? And if in the land of peace, in which you trusted, they wearied you, then how will you do in the floodplain of the Jordan?" (Jer. 12:5). Could it be that apostolic leaders and the Church are unprepared for what is coming? *Leader!* will seek to overcome unpreparedness in leadership by looking at qualities and characteristics, strengths and weaknesses, and the hardships of being chosen by God to be an end-time leader. In turn, apostles and other leaders will then guide the body of Christ.

This book is a "must-read" for apostolic leaders. *Leader!* is a companion to *The Strategy of Knowledge!*

No Shame Zone
Exposing the Hidden Bondage of Shame

Lack of recognition is the biggest problem for eliminating shame. Many who are burdened by shame do not even realize the name for the intense emotion that they feel. The effects of shame are also found throughout the pages of Scripture. In fact, the first negative emotion from the first sin was shame! Satan used that vile trick immediately with Adam and Eve in the Garden of Eden! That fact alone says something about the strength of the weapon of shame in Satan's hands. The Lord Jesus Christ has revealed eye-opening biblical truths to expose shame. It is a huge problem for those in the Church, as well as for those who do not yet have a relationship with Jesus Christ.

No Shame Zone
Discussion and Study Guide
Exposing the Hidden Bondage of Shame and Effectively Dealing with It!

The *NO SHAME ZONE DISCUSSION AND STUDY GUIDE* was written to complement *NO SHAME ZONE,* a book about exposing the hidden bondage of shame. The heart of the matter is to help people effectively deal with shame so they may walk in freedom. The questions contained in the *NO SHAME ZONE DISCUSSION AND STUDY GUIDE* are meant to stir thoughts and to provoke new ways to consider old problems. The Bible will provide all needed answers to the questions posed! This manual has many suggested verses to point to godly discernment of shame, unforgiveness, embarrassment, hurt, repentance, and other topics.

Who is the Bride?
A Mandate for the Church for Such a Time as This!

Did you ever wonder why the Church struggles to walk in the blessing of the Lord that is promised in Scripture? Have you questioned why the Church grapples for relevance in the culture where evil is running amok? The Lord promised that those who bless Israel will be blessed and those who curse Israel will be cursed. The Church must understand the biblical mandate to appeal to the King of kings for the salvation of the Jews. The inclusion of the Jews as a part of the bride of Christ will loose blessing and favor of the Lord on the Church.

Kingdom Citizenship Now!
Experience God's Kingdom on Earth as it is in Heaven!

When God's presence and power come on earth, miracles happen. Learn why miracles happen. Investigate what hinders the kingdom of God from fully manifesting on earth. Understand what believers can do to invite the unending power of God on earth as it is in heaven. *Kingdom Citizenship Now!* is full of new revelations and scriptural understanding. This book has over 900 biblical references. *Kingdom Citizenship Now!* is a vessel of God for new understanding into the meaning of even well-known passages. Experience God's kingdom on earth, NOW!

Salvation is Free, Discipleship is Not!
Weighing the Cost of NOT Serving God!

Salvation is Free, Discipleship is Not! Weighing the Cost of NOT Serving God! is a cry to the Church of Jesus Christ to experience a wake up call. Time is short! The Church is called to wake up and be in a state of preparation and readiness for the return of the Lord. Jesus Christ is returning for a Bride who has made herself ready to meet her Groom. The body of Christ is drowsy or may have already fallen asleep. Sadly, some who think they are ready to meet Jesus will be mistaken. There will be many who hear those terrifying words, "Truly I tell you, I don't know you" (Matt. 25:12). The Lord is not willing that any should perish. Scripture is very plain, however, that there are those who have confessed Christ with their mouths, but who have not known him in their hearts. They will be sent away into eternal damnation.

CPSIA information can be obtained
at www.ICGtesting.com
Printed in the USA
FFOW03n0401140118
44504178-44331FF